Integrating Social and Emotional Learning with Content

Integrating Social and Emotional Learning with Content builds a framework for creatively and effectively using picture books to integrate social and emotional learning (SEL) with teaching across content areas.

Thoughtful book choices in mixed-ability early elementary classrooms have the power to not only support gifted students as they develop academically, but also to provide an opportunity to address their unique social and emotional needs, such as asynchronous development and an early awareness of complex and challenging issues in their lives and the world at large. Picture books are an invaluable tool for this work because the characters, topics, and settings increasingly represent and celebrate the lived experiences of diverse student populations, supporting culturally responsive teaching.

Packed with lesson plans, book lists, and more, this book is perfect for teachers in gifted and mixed-ability classrooms as well as homeschooling parents looking to help their children make meaningful connections between their culture, languages, and lived experiences and the academic content and SEL skills they are being taught in the classroom.

Katherine Kapustka is a program leader and associate professor of elementary education at DePaul University, where she teaches a variety of classes in the elementary education program, including literacy and assessment. In her research and writing, she draws upon her prior experience as a fifth-grade teacher, her current work with pre-service teachers, and the knowledge gained as she raises her two children.

Sarah Bright is a post-doctoral research associate at Purdue University, where she works on a research project that focuses on closing opportunity gaps for students from traditionally underserved populations in gifted education in STEM domains. Her broader research interests include social and emotional learning in elementary gifted settings and the impact of instructional technology within gifted education.

Integrating Social and Emotional Learning with Content

Using Picture Books for Differentiated Teaching in K-3 Classrooms

Katherine Kapustka and Sarah Bright

NEW YORK AND LONDON

Cover image credits: © Getty Images

First published 2022
by Routledge
605 Third Avenue, New York, NY 10158

and by Routledge
2 Park Square, Milton Park, Abingdon, Oxon, OX14 4RN

Routledge is an imprint of the Taylor & Francis Group, an informa business

© 2022 Katherine Kapustka and Sarah Bright

The right of Katherine Kapustka and Sarah Bright to be identified as authors of this work has been asserted in accordance with sections 77 and 78 of the Copyright, Designs and Patents Act 1988.

All rights reserved. No part of this book may be reprinted or reproduced or utilised in any form or by any electronic, mechanical, or other means, now known or hereafter invented, including photocopying and recording, or in any information storage or retrieval system, without permission in writing from the publishers.

Trademark notice: Product or corporate names may be trademarks or registered trademarks, and are used only for identification and explanation without intent to infringe.

Library of Congress Cataloging-in-Publication Data
A catalog record for this book has been requested

ISBN: 978-1-032-16186-0 (hbk)
ISBN: 978-1-032-14920-2 (pbk)
ISBN: 978-1-003-24742-5 (ebk)

DOI: 10.4324/9781003247425

Typeset in Palatino
by Apex CoVantage, LLC

Contents

Acknowledgements vi

Introduction 1

1 Social and Emotional Learning and Gifted
  Children 7

2 Choosing Quality Picture Books 30

3 Matching Children to Books 48

4 Integrating SEL and Subject Content in
  Lesson Plans 61

5 Integrating SEL and STEM Using Picture Books 86

6 Integrating SEL and Social Studies Using
  Picture Books 118

7 Integrating SEL and ELA Using Literary Texts 150

8 Integrating SEL and ELA Using
  Informational Texts 172

  Conclusion: Using Picture Books to Build a
  Lesson Plan 195

Acknowledgements

We are deeply grateful for the many people who have offered support, advice, and encouragement throughout the writing process:

Our local librarians, Jess Alexander and the children's librarians at the Morton Grove Public Library, who suggested so many beautiful books and ways of looking at SEL for younger readers. The multiple branches of the Aurora Public Library were an invaluable resource as well, including the librarians and the staff who manage the process of moving books between branches and labeling them for pickup!

The teachers at Science and Arts Academy in Des Plaines, particularly Tina Centineo, whose SEL lessons and book collection were an inspiration, and Linda Spataro, who generously shared her lessons and suggestions for incorporating SEL in STEM.

The faculty, staff, and students at DePaul University who taught us, challenged us, and encouraged us along this journey.

Roxanne Owens, the chair of the Department of Teacher Education, who was kind enough to read our original prospectus and has been an invaluable support for our work ever since.

Mary Hynes-Berry, who graciously shared her knowledge about the power of bibliotherapy and suggested many resources that guided our thinking on the connections between texts and SEL.

Finally, writing a book during a pandemic, with our children in various stages of online, hybrid, and in-person learning, would never have been possible without the support of our families. They provided encouragement and feedback, graciously maneuvered around the piles of pictures books we brought home (or occasionally picked them up to read and review), and, especially in the final few weeks of the writing process, took responsibility for more than their fair share of household chores. We thank you for your love and support.

Introduction

A first-grade student writes a note to her teacher asking: "Please, if it wouldn't be too much trouble, could I get some more challenging work during reading time?" Just a few miles away, another first grader draws detailed constellations on his blue jeans during science class and then crawls under his desk when the teacher scolds him for not following along with the lesson. These children, both formally identified as "gifted" by their school districts in later years, struggle throughout elementary school to find the intellectual stimulation and social and emotional support they need to have their educational needs met in their general education classrooms. Similar stories undoubtedly play out daily in schools of all types. Some have no formal programs for gifted students and rely entirely on differentiation in general education classrooms. Others may wait until third or fourth grade to provide gifted services, possibly through a "pull out" model. Yet others may be "gifted" schools or classrooms, with early identification of students and placements in self-contained environments with other gifted children. While every educational environment has its own set of challenges, in each, classroom teachers may struggle to meet the academic and social and emotional needs of their gifted students, particularly in schools where standards-based curricula and external accountability assessments add to the already complex job of being a classroom teacher. There are so many requirements placed on teachers, and most have become quite adept at finding innovative ways to address the items on their "to-do lists." This book serves as one additional resource, as it provides a framework for understanding how to meet the needs of gifted students, and all students, in any given classroom, through the integration of social and emotional learning (SEL) with learning in the content-areas and English Language Arts (ELA), using diverse picture books as the base for instruction.

Differentiation and Integration

Students come into classrooms with a variety of unique academic and social and emotional needs. They have different language, cultural, and educational backgrounds that impact their current levels of educational attainment, as well as inform the types of educational environments and experiences that will best help them progress. In addition to the differences in academic interests and abilities, students also have different social and emotional strengths and challenges. It is not rare to find children in classrooms who perform several years beyond their typically developing peers in one or more content areas but struggle to find friends or regulate their behaviors to meet the expectations of the school environment. In a general education classroom, there will be students who need assistance and support to catch up academically to their peers, and these students, too, will exhibit a range of social and emotional competencies. For this reason, teachers must be able to differentiate their instruction to meet the needs of all students in the classroom.

Additionally, in many schools throughout the nation, all curricula are expected to be standards-based. In some cases, these are national standards, like the Common Core State Standards for English Language Arts and Mathematics or the Next Generation Science Standards, while in other cases they are designed at the state level. Even private schools may emphasize meeting specific learning standards. Teachers may also be required to administer external accountability tests to determine students' progress toward these standards, and in some cases, teacher evaluation, including tenure and raises, may be tied to students' performances on these assessments.

Added to the pressures to meet specific academic standards, educators are increasingly coming to understand the importance of developing students' social and emotional skills, both for enhanced learning in the classroom, but, more importantly, success throughout life. While versions of SEL have been around for decades (e.g., character education, emotional intelligence, peace education, restorative justice), it is only recently that educators have come to realize that these practices are all rooted in the frameworks for and research on SEL (Tate, 2019). In addition, an increase in the number of elementary-aged children diagnosed with mental health conditions, including anxiety and depression, has placed the issue of SEL in the forefront of many educators' minds.

This book suggests a framework that uses picture books as the basis for integrating SEL with learning in ELA, science, and social studies, with a specific emphasis on differentiating to meet the needs of gifted learners. This framework is powerful for all teaching situations, and it can be applied in work with students in a variety of teaching contexts. For example, a teacher may be working with students who demonstrate many characteristics of giftedness but have not yet been identified, or perhaps they have not scored high enough on qualifying tests to be admitted formally to a gifted program. Maybe there are no gifted services available, or the child is "twice-exceptional" and has an area of disability that is masking the giftedness. This framework can also meet the needs of students who are academically "on target" and those who struggle academically, as a variety of differentiation options are included in each content-area and ELA chapter.

Picture Books

This is an exciting time for educators interested in using children's books that represent a wide range of differences. Teachers who are searching for books that represent the range of diversities in their classroom (e.g., ethnic, cultural, linguistic, religious, socio-economic, familial, dis/ability) are likely to find at least some options in their school or local libraries or through major publishers. Data from the Cooperative Children's Book Center at the University of Wisconsin-Madison shows that in all categories (Black/African, Indigenous, Asian, Latinx, Pacific Islander, and Arab) the percentages of children's books that are written about and/or by people of color has increased over time, although there is still much work to be done. As a classroom teacher, finding books that serve as a "mirror" of the lived experiences of the students in the classroom and a "window" to see the lives of people who are quite different has never been easier.

Picture books are a powerful tool for use in any elementary classroom in a variety of subject areas. In both literary and informational texts, children may see young people who look like them or live in similar circumstances. These books may provide support and connection for students experiencing difficulties, but also inspiration to encourage children to think beyond their immediate circumstances. Well-written picture books, through the power of storytelling, can transport children to different eras and places, and into the lives of people who are at times very similar to (and at others, very different from) themselves. On a purely practical level, picture books are often easily accessible and affordable. Teachers can find them in school and local libraries, as well as through digital platforms. Also, because of the abundance of picture books available, teachers can find books on a common topic or theme at a variety of reading levels.

In writing this book, we have reviewed many hundreds of books. Many we liked, some we loved, and a small number we sent back almost immediately to our local libraries. In choosing books to highlight in subsequent chapters, we focused on books that succeed in balancing a compelling narrative with instructional content. There are numerous books that lean more heavily toward instruction, for example explaining to children how to manage their emotions through meditation or describing what a democracy is. You will not find many of these books on our lists. Instead, you will find books that guide students in thinking about SEL competencies while at same time supporting content-area and ELA learning. In addition, we have endeavored to highlight books that reflect the diversity in our society and that appeal to us as readers and as educators. We present these books as suggestions, but we also encourage you to consider the schools and communities in which you work and to choose the books that fit your individual contexts.

Overview of the Book

In education today there is an increasing focus on meeting the unique academic and social and emotional needs of all students;

at the same time teachers are being asked to align their teaching with content area standards and, often, external accountability assessments. Teachers are challenged to attend to all of these demands with no increase in the length of the school day or extra support for their endeavors. For these reasons, this book provides concrete suggestions in the form of lesson ideas, suggestions for differentiation, and book lists, all of which can be easily adapted or modified to meet a teacher's specific context and curriculum.

The next three chapters of this book provide a foundation for understanding how and why to integrate content-area and ELA learning with SEL, using picture books as the guiding material. Chapter 1 describes the main components of SEL, with specific consideration of bibliotherapy, a technique used to promote healing and personal growth in children. Chapter 2 focuses on understanding how to identify quality picture books, since these books will be at the heart of the lessons. Chapter 3 addresses the complexities of matching children to books, specifically referencing some of the unique challenges that teachers may face when working with gifted students. The second section of the book, Chapters 4–8, focuses on specific techniques and examples for putting these ideas into place in the classroom. Chapter 4 provides an overview of the framework for integration and differentiation, and then Chapters 5–8 consider how to use these techniques in science, technology, engineering and math, social studies, and ELA with literary and informational texts. The book ends with a conclusion that provides an overview of key concepts and an encouragement to continue with the complex work of designing truly integrated, differentiated learning experiences that meet the needs of all learners.

Notes to Our Readers

Throughout the book, we use the terms *educators* and *teachers* interchangeably. We anticipate that most of the readers of this book will be classroom teachers or future teachers in the fields of early childhood, elementary, and gifted education, but we have endeavored to appeal to and meet the needs of other school professionals involved in the intellectual and social and emotional development of children. These may include administrators, librarians, counselors, and social workers, as well as those who work in more informal settings such as camps and after-school programs, and parents and caregivers who may be interested in supporting their children's academic and social and emotional development at home.

When referring to the authors, Sarah and Katherine (Kathie), will use the term *we*. We use this pronoun to indicate our combined personal and professional opinions. In the rare instances where something applies to only one of us, we will use our first names.

Throughout this book, we have chosen to use the Common Core State Standards and the national standards for science and social studies because of their broad reach. Where other standards are in use, we are confident that you will find significant overlap between the standards referenced in this book and the topics, themes, and skills found in the standards that are in place in your particular context.

Finally, when considering gifted learners and differentiation, we use the term *gifted* to refer to all students who are in need of an academic challenge, whether they have been formally identified or not. In the early chapters that provide a foundation for this book, you will find the needs of gifted learners considered explicitly. In the later chapters, the examples and lesson plans are designed to meet all learners' needs in mixed-ability classrooms. We realize that this includes a broad range of students, and as you think about meeting the specific needs of gifted students, we hope that you will consider addition options, such as full-grade and subject-area acceleration, among others.

References

Cooperative Children's Book Center, School of Education, University of Wisconsin-Madison. (n.d.). *Books by and/or about Black, Indigenous and People of Color 2018*. https://ccbc.education.wisc.edu/literature-resources/ccbc-diversity-statistics/books-by-and-or-about-poc-2018/.

Tate, E. (2019, May 7). Why social-emotional learning is suddenly in the spotlight. *EdSurge Podcast*. www.edsurge.com/news/2019-05-07-why-social-emotional-learning-is-suddenly-in-the-spotlight.

1

Social and Emotional Learning and Gifted Children

Throughout popular culture, highly creative and intelligent people are often portrayed as socially and psychologically abnormal, through stories of wild-eyed wizards and obsessive scientists, and in depictions of highly talented but unstable artists and scholars such as the manic Amadeus Mozart, the tormented and suicidal Van Gogh, and the schizophrenic and delusional mathematician John Nash. Gifted children such as *A Wrinkle in Time*'s Charles Wallace, Roald Dahl's Matilda, and the child team in the Mysterious Benedict Society series are brainy outcasts who struggle for acceptance, often working on secret plans to foil dastardly plots (Stewart, 2007). Evil geniuses in such works as Eoin Colfer's Artemis Fowl series, Catherine Jinks' Evil Genius series, and Josh Lieb's *I Am a Genius of Unspeakable Evil and I Want to Be Your Class President* are complex social misfits who turn to malicious destruction.

Research on gifted and talented children has disproven the popular myth of gifted children as brilliant but troubled pariahs and demonstrated that gifted students are overall well-adjusted, psychologically healthy children who have unique talents and abilities (Neihart & Yeo, 2018; Reis & Renzulli, 2004; Robinson, 2002). The solution to addressing those students' need for differentiated curriculum and content includes options such as accelerated or compacted curriculum, grade-skipping, and the use of extension activities to allow the students to delve more deeply into topics of interest. But the research on the impact of exceptional talent on children's social and emotional traits and needs is more complicated. Despite the fact that gifted students are psychologically and emotionally stable, negative stereotypes and perceptions of difference stemming from gifted students' needs and behaviors drive a distance between them and their peers. Some teachers are uncertain about how to help gifted students in mixed-ability classrooms, leaving them to work on their own or putting them in a role of teachers' assistant, further isolating them from their classmates.

What is the best way to support these students, their peers, and their teachers from a social and emotional perspective? Recent research helps us examine questions such as: Are there emotional or psychological characteristics unique to gifted students? Do gifted students need particular social and emotional support and programs, and if so, which ones are most effective? How can educators, families, and communities support gifted students in ways that foster their growth and include them within their communities?

A helpful way to examine these questions for all students—not only those who are gifted or show high potential—is through the framework of social and emotional learning (SEL), which is the process of fostering students' emotional, social, and cognitive skills to help them build healthy self-concepts, manage relationships and conflicts, and develop skills to navigate challenges in personal, social, and academic situations. Educators, mental health professionals, community and family members, and others in child support roles use SEL to build up the skills that children need to navigate challenging situations, either within their own lives or in their experiences with friends or classmates. Social and emotional learning is appropriate from the earliest ages, in school and home settings, and embedded within all curriculum and content.

In this chapter we will provide a definition of social and emotional learning and give an overview of the most-cited SEL frameworks in K-12 schools. Although there are no national SEL standards, an increasing number of states are including SEL outcomes alongside their own standards. We will summarize research on the use and effectiveness of social and emotional learning programs in the general school setting and specifically within the gifted and talented community, addressing questions regarding the differences and unique needs of gifted students. Narrowing our focus to younger students, we will discuss ways to support social and emotional learning in elementary schools. We will conclude with an explanation of the use of picture books to support gifted students socially and emotionally within an academic setting, guiding them as they make meaningful connections between their culture, languages, and lived experiences.

What Is Social and Emotional Learning?

Social and emotional learning (SEL) comprises three parts: social SEL skills, emotional SEL skills, and cognitive SEL skills. Social SEL skills help students understand and respond in challenging social situations and interpersonal conflicts, work cooperatively, and demonstrate positive emotions such as kindness and empathy toward others. Emotional SEL skills allow students to develop emotional intelligence, which helps them to understand and navigate their own emotions and recognize and appropriately respond to other people's feelings and points of view. Cognitive SEL skills include executive functioning abilities, such as planning, prioritization and completion of tasks, working memory, self-regulation and inhibitory control, and flexibility (Cramer & Castro-Olivo, 2016; Hamilton, 2020). Each skill has developmentally appropriate milestones that build on one another and grow more focused at higher grades (Jones et al., 2017). For example, social skills for younger children include understanding and communicating emotions, which is necessary for children's interactions beginning at the earliest ages. By middle and high school, navigating and communicating emotions is a highly complex process wrapped up in adolescent physical, social, and academic challenges.

The term *social and emotional learning* was coined at a 1994 meeting of researchers, educators, and children's mental health advocates hosted by the Fetzer Institute, and the Collaborative for Academic, Social, and Emotional Learning (CASEL) was also established that year with the goal of creating rigorous, research-based, social emotional programs in all K-12 schools (CASEL, n.d.). Several CASEL publications, including *Promoting Social and Emotional Learning: Guidelines for Educators* (1997), co-authored by the Association for Supervision and Curriculum Development, and the 2015 *Handbook of Social and Emotional Learning: Research and Practice* detail the research and best practices for implementing SEL programs throughout schools.

Numerous large-scale, longitudinal studies completed since the widespread adoption of SEL programs in the 1990s have proven the positive impact of social and emotional learning on a wide array of children's social-emotional skills, classroom behavior and attitudes, and well-being indicators such as a stable self-concept and stress management (Taylor et al., 2017). In addition to positive impacts on social-emotional competencies and grade-school preparation, an Australian study found that a structured 10-week SEL program resulted in an increase in the reading achievement scores of struggling first graders (Ashdown & Bernard, 2012). The impacts of SEL programs are long-lasting; a Brookings Institute study found that SEL programming can have a positive impact for up to 18 years on students' academics, social competence, conduct problems, emotional distress, and drug use (CASEL, n.d.; Conduct Problems Prevention Research Group, 2010; Durlak & Mahoney, 2019).

Frameworks for SEL

The number of SEL frameworks and their concentrations are constantly expanding, and several organizations have analyzed and provided inventories of the frameworks and their competencies and domains. The American Institutes for Research completed a wide-ranging analysis of 136 SEL frameworks for ages 6 to 25, looking at more than 20 areas of study, including school-based competency development, mindfulness, resilience, and public health, then compiling their competencies and measures (Berg et al., 2017). Harvard University's Explore SEL project maintains an online database of more than 40 widely adopted SEL frameworks in a variety of disciplines. The Explore SEL project uses six domains of SEL to categorize the frameworks:

- **Cognitive**, which includes developing executive functioning skills such as goal setting, task initiation, and time management; good decision-making; problem-solving and working through challenges; and learning from failure
- **Emotion**, which includes the understanding, expression, and control of students' own emotions, and the interpretation and appropriate responses to other children's emotions
- **Social**, which includes communicating, playing, and interacting with others, and understanding and managing conflicts in a healthy way
- **Values**, which include the development of ethical values, character traits, and habits that position a child to be a compassionate person who contributes to their community and world in positive ways
- **Perspectives**, which include nurturing such outlooks as optimism, courage, gratitude, and hope; developing a growth mindset, grit, and perseverance; expanding self-confidence and willingness to step outside of comfort zones; and welcoming mentoring to grow from critiques and criticism
- **Identity**, which includes building a healthy self-awareness, self-efficacy, and sense of identity and place in the world, and fostering an understanding of the diversity of identities within local and global communities

These six domains cover aspects of social and emotional competencies and skills from broad categories such as core academic skills to specific traits such as flexibility and stress tolerance. The Explore SEL website (http://exploresel.gse.harvard.edu/), which is regularly updated to include new frameworks, also includes a frameworks profile tool that allows users to compare frameworks across multiple domains to show commonalities and differences among the frameworks.

Implementation of SEL standards at the state level is increasing. In a 2018 analysis, CASEL found that 14 states have specific K-12 SEL standards, and an additional 11 states have resource and guidance documents (CASEL, n.d.). The CASEL framework (Figure 1.1) is cited by 10 out of 14 of the states with specified SEL standards and provides the foundation or key aspects for other SEL standards that have been developed

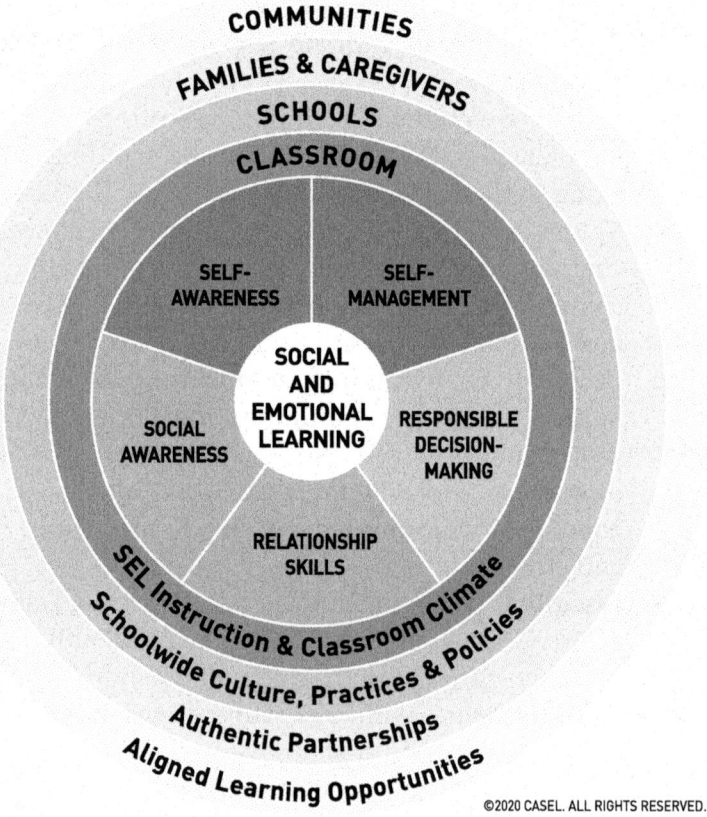

FIGURE 1.1 The CASEL Wheel of Social & Emotional Learning
Source: © 2020 CASEL. All Rights Reserved. https://casel.org/fundamentals-of-sel/what-is-the-casel-framework/

by the states (CASEL, n.d.). It includes five key SEL competencies: self-awareness (e.g., understanding the impact of emotions and action), self-management (e.g., managing emotions and behavior), social awareness (e.g., understanding the perspectives and circumstances of other people and institutions), relationship skills (e.g., establishing healthy and supportive relationships), and responsible decision-making (CASEL, 2020). The framework shows four areas of implementation: in the classroom, where SEL can be embedded in the curriculum and in the climate of the classroom; in schools, where administrators implement consistent policies and support in all areas; by families and caregivers; and in the communities through aligned learning opportunities with schools and families. The coordination of all four areas of SEL implementation helps to ensure an inclusive culture and consistent application of the SEL policies (Mahoney et al., 2020).

Harvard's Explore SEL domains and the CASEL framework taken together provide a picture of the skills, abilities, mindsets, and outlooks that comprise a fully realized and participating individual in our society—one who is aware of themselves, their views and impacts, and their responsibilities within their community and the world as a whole. In this book we will cite domains and competencies from both Harvard's Explore SEL and CASEL's frameworks.

Social and Emotional Learning With Gifted Students

Research into the psychosocial backgrounds of gifted children dates from the 1920s, when Louis Terman's 1925 longitudinal study of more than 1,000 high-IQ children, Catherine Cox's 1926 book *The Early Mental Traits of Three Hundred Geniuses*, and Leta Stetter Hollingworth's *Gifted Children: Their Nature and Nurture* (1926) marked the beginning of an effort to portray gifted and talented people as fully functioning and well-adjusted individuals and to understand their social and emotional needs (Neihart, 1999; Rinn, 2018). The question of whether gifted and talented students have greater social emotional needs and challenges than the overall student population has been discussed and studied at length. The most recent research supports three main conclusions: first, gifted students are as equally likely as non-gifted students to experience challenging life experiences and emotional struggles, such as the divorce or loss of parents, conflicts with their peers, substance abuse, neglect, and anxiety and depression, so they should be supported in facing and managing those experiences as all students should (Moon, 2009). However, gifted children are not more likely to have psychological problems and mental illnesses than the general student population (Preckel et al., 2015). Finally, gifted and talented children do have unique challenges stemming from complexities that arise as they navigate school and social settings as students with abilities that are different from their peers (Neihart & Yeo, 2018), and the students need support to navigate those challenges.

The research and popular beliefs around the social and emotional needs of gifted and talented children focus on five key topics: overexcitabilities, asynchronous development, motivation, perfectionism, and self-concept. In each of these cases, there is some evidence for a higher occurrence or impact with gifted students as well as misunderstandings and overestimations of their effects that have an impact on the programs and attitudes used with gifted students. We will address the common misconceptions and research regarding each of these in the following sections.

Overexcitabilities

One of the most controversial topics in gifted psychology is the theory of overexcitabilities, behaviors in which a person's response is greater than a typical response to stimuli. The theory of overexcitabilities was presented by Polish psychologist Kazimierz Dabrowski, who defined five specific types of overexcitabilities: psychomotor, sensual, intellectual, imaginational, and emotional. Some researchers and educators argue that overexcitabilities are both unique characteristics and defining attributes of giftedness (Daniels & Piechowski, 2009; Silverman, 2000). They cite examples of overexcitabilities in gifted students' high physical energy and intense emotions, heightened sensitivity in the five senses, daydreaming and creation of imaginative and fantasy playscapes, and deep curiosity and a drive to delve deeply into complex issues and questions (Lamont, 2012).

Dabrowski's overexcitabilities are a small part of his broader, complex theory of psychological and personality development called positive disintegration (Gross, Rinn, & Jamieson, 2007; Harrison & Van Haneghan, 2011). Research regarding whether overexcitabilities are more common in the gifted population is mixed, and recent research cautions against using Dabrowski's theory of overexcitabilities with gifted students apart from his broader theory of positive disintegration (Mendaglio, 2012; Tillier, 2009). The use of overexcitabilities to explain gifted students' behavior risks masking anxiety disorders, ADHD, or other psychological challenges that should be addressed separately (Kane, 2009).

Social and emotional learning tools help students with perceived overexcitabilities such as intense emotions, which fall under the CASEL competencies of self-awareness and self-management, and obsessive focus on tasks or topics, which is included in the Harvard cognitive domain of executive functioning skills and time management.

Asynchronous Development

A widely referenced challenge for gifted students is asynchronous development, which is the development of gifted students' cognitive, emotional, and physical abilities and traits at different paces (NAGC, n.d.; Silverman, 2002). Examples include gifted students' higher abilities in one subject over another, and students who have more advanced cognitive skills but fall behind their peers in fine motor control abilities.

Gifted students can experience asynchronous development between their aptitudes and ages, resulting in challenges in making friends with similar abilities and interests (APA, 2017; Neihart & Yeo, 2018). This difference is greatest among exceptionally and profoundly gifted students (with IQs of more than 160 and 180, respectively) and in younger children, who have not yet developed the social skills and emotional knowledge to navigate social situations and build friendships (Neihart & Yeo, 2018). An example of asynchronous development in early childhood and elementary grades can occur when a child develops interests that are more complex or beyond the typical level of interest of children their age, leaving them socially isolated in conversations about their interests or in make-believe games. SEL tools in the social and emotional domains address challenges of asynchronous development, including effectively communicating and interacting with other children, building a healthy self-awareness, and defining their identity.

Motivation

Motivation is a key topic in discussions of giftedness because high motivation is often considered to be both a common characteristic of giftedness (Gagné, 2005a; Renzulli, 2005) and a necessary trait for gifted students to be able to develop their talents and reach their potential (Subotnik, Olszewski-Kubilius & Worrell, 2011). However, unhealthy or maladaptive motivation can lead to anxiety, depression, and unhealthy perfectionism. Gifted research breaks motivation into the categories of extrinsic motivation, which is motivation driven by external factors such as parental expectations or peer pressure and the promise of rewards, and intrinsic motivation, which is driven by internal pressure and the reward of completion (Rinn & Majority, 2018). Gifted students generally have more intrinsic than extrinsic motivation (McCoach & Flake, 2018), which drives a sense of autonomy and need to feel competent in relation to their peers (Clinkenbeard, 2012). SEL tools regarding healthy motivation focus on the domains of emotion and perspective, and on self-awareness, helping students manage their motivations to keep them as positive forces and encouragement rather than harmful or negative impediments to students' success and happiness.

Perfectionism

Like motivation, perfectionism in gifted students can be a benefit or an obstacle. Striving for perfection in the form of high achievement acts as a motivator to many students who seek success and the mastery of difficult skills or content, such as a musical ability that requires extensive practice. Helpful perfectionism can foster creativity, problem-solving, and even support life satisfaction and longevity, while negative perfectionism holds a person to impossible standards and may result in depression, anxiety, and low self-concept (Rice & Taber, 2018; Schuler, 2002). Young students with maladaptive perfectionism who cannot achieve the goals they set for themselves could end up underachieving or struggling with task completion. While there is a widely held belief that gifted students are more prone to negative perfectionism, research has found that there is a complex relationship between perfectionism and social and emotional happiness, and the impacts vary among countries (Rice & Taber, 2018). SEL tools that help students manage perfectionism are in the same areas as the SEL tools for motivation: the CASEL competency of self-awareness and the Harvard domains of emotion and perspective.

Self-Concept/Identity

The development of a positive sense of self-concept is crucial to the success and healthy adjustment of all students, but it is particularly important for gifted students whose identities and places in the world may feel different from that of their friends and peers. Research has found conflicting evidence of gifted children's self-concept, with evidence of both higher and lower self-concept among gifted students than their peers (Shechtman & Silektor, 2012). One commonly discussed phenomenon in gifted education is the "big-fish-little-pond effect," in which gifted students have high self-concept in mixed-ability classes in which they are at the highest level of achievement, but when put in a class with peers of equal or higher ability they suffer from low self-concept (Marsh et al., 2007; Marsh & Craven, 2000).

An important aspect of self-concept is the students' sense of their identity within the gifted community and the student population overall. The demographic of the gifted student population has an overrepresentation of affluent White and Asian students in comparison with the general population; Black, Latinx, and Native American students, and students of lower socioeconomic status are underrepresented in gifted programs in proportion to their representation in the general student population (Peters & Engerrand, 2016; Siegle et al., 2016). The result of this is that the students who are in the minority often do not fit into the standard assumptions and representations of identity of gifted students. They may not find themselves with similar peers in their gifted programs. Further, gifted content and curricula often does not include characters and content that are culturally similar to minoritized gifted students' lives and experiences, with the result that both the content materials and the experiences they have in the classroom are not similar to their own backgrounds and experiences.

Gender and sexual self-identification of gifted students and the danger of stereotyped gender norms regarding the interests, behaviors, and expectations of gifted students also play an important role in their identity. There is limited research regarding LGBTQ gifted youth, but the pressures, abuse, and misunderstandings that LGBTQ youth suffer from in the general student population may be compounded by stresses of exclusion or misunderstanding in the gifted population (Cohn, 2002; NAGC, n.d.). The combination of inaccurate representation, hurtful stereotypes, and lack of research and support can result in challenges for LGBTQ youth in establishing a healthy self-concept.

SEL domains that are relevant to self-concept include CASEL's self-awareness domain and Harvard's identity domain. Reinforcement of confidence, self-expression, and self-efficacy are important tools to foster for healthy self-concept, and the use of culturally relevant pedagogy and curriculum with all students throughout the school is a vital component of SEL and an illustration of the use of SEL within the school setting on the CASEL framework.

Supporting SEL in the Gifted Population Through a Talent Development Perspective

Tying in with the historical belief of a correlation between high ability and psychosocial differences, much of the research and discussion around the social and emotional needs of gifted students use a deficit perspective that focuses on the challenges and shortcomings that gifted students need to overcome. Articles by educators, researchers, and medical practitioners offer advice about SEL interventions with deficit language around alleviating gifted children's fears and anxieties, overcoming their negative emotions, and changing their aggressive and hostile attitudes and behaviors. The use of a deficit perspective assumes that gifted students start at an inferior status and need to grow and heal to be at a healthy level with their peers, a belief that is not supported by research regarding the psychosocial status of gifted students.

A more accurate and appropriate approach uses a talent development perspective (Gagné, 2005b; Olszewski-Kubilius & Calvert, 2015; Olszewski-Kubilius, Subotnik, & Worrell, 2018; Subotnik et al., 2011) that looks at how educators can most effectively prepare students to develop the skills they need to succeed, find their identity, and establish a healthy self-concept. The use of a talent development framework also broadens the social and emotional focus beyond the individual child to make it relevant within their community and globally. In addition to supporting the individual child, educators should focus on looking at the social contexts and cultural systems that label the child deficient (Hoffman, 2009). Using the talent development perspective, the lessons and language of SEL tools should focus on recognizing growth and opportunities, celebrating achievements and milestones, encouraging progress, reaching beyond a student's comfort zone, and taking on challenges with a positive mindset.

Implementing SEL Programs in Schools and Classrooms

Though the specific emphases differ among SEL standards and frameworks, the most common overarching recommendations for K-12 SEL standards are that the SEL content and pedagogy should be differentiated, inclusive, and presented repeatedly in multiple contexts throughout the students' learning experiences (APA, 2017). A limitation of many SEL programs is that they are administered as single, stand-alone lessons given once a week or less. Such small doses of SEL instruction have limited effect because SEL skills, like academic skills, develop over time and require continuous implementation in multiple settings (Jones & Bouffard, 2012).

CASEL recommends that the content and pedagogy of the social and emotional learning programs be customized for the cognitive, emotional, and social needs of the students, and state that the programs should be adjusted over time to fit the children's changing developmental abilities and needs (Jones et al., 2017). SEL programs should be relevant to all children's cultural, linguistic, socioeconomic, gender, and sexual identities (Hoffman, 2009; Neihart & Yeo, 2018), so that all students feel engaged, empowered, and included. Such concepts as ability, self-concept, and happiness and well-being should be presented within every student's specific cultural contexts, and those contexts should be shared universally, fostering understanding and empathy among students. The American Institutes for Research (AIR) study of 136 frameworks found that the overwhelming majority did not tailor their frameworks for culturally and linguistically diverse individuals, disabled youth, or children and adolescents who have suffered trauma (Berg, 2017), a serious shortcoming that should be addressed by educators and administrators. To address that shortcoming, the recommendations for lessons and books provided here are aimed at providing support for a diverse range of students.

Social and Emotional Learning Applications and Programs in Elementary Grades

As with any curriculum, the expectations and outcomes for social and emotional learning vary based on age, grade, and ability level. The CASEL framework does not provide grade-level performance indicators or competencies, but many organizations have used the CASEL framework to create grade-level learning benchmarks and performance descriptors. Dusenbury et al. (2015) list two key SEL competencies for the elementary grades: students should be able to independently negotiate and manage peer relationships, friendships, and conflicts; and students should be able to demonstrate appropriate emotions in a variety of contexts. The state of Illinois, for example, created three SEL goals with performance descriptors and benchmarks at five grade-level clusters. Their three SEL goals, which share key concepts with the CASEL competencies, are: develop self-awareness and self-management skills to achieve school and life success; use social-awareness and interpersonal skills to establish and maintain positive relationships; and demonstrate decision-making skills and responsible behaviors in personal, school, and community contexts. At the early elementary grades the performance descriptors include having children identify their own emotions and the emotions of characters in their stories, describe ways to manage a conflict, and identify values that help in good decision-making (Illinois State Board of Education, n.d.).

In the lower elementary grades, instructional practices for teaching social and emotional learning include discussions; didactic instruction; book and story readings; vocabulary exercises; writing assignments; drawing, art, and creative projects; visual displays; videos; songs; role-playing; games; and movement-based activities (Jones et al., 2017). Teachers can organize the students into small groups to facilitate collaboration skills and use the "RULER" skills of SEL (Recognizing, Understanding, Labeling, Expressing, and Regulating emotions) to help foster emotional skills and values such as respect, self-awareness, perspective-taking, and empathy. Students share their own feeling words, such as *happy*, *angry*, *sad*, *disappointed*, and *frustrated*, or read a story and label the characters' feelings (Dusenbury et al., 2015; Nathanson et al., 2016). The 4R program (Reading, Writing, Respect, and Resolution) uses book talks and read-alouds to teach such SEL skills as empathy, conflict management, and respecting diversity (Oberle & Schonert-Reichl, 2017).

To take a specific example of implementation, CASEL gives examples of SEL programs that teach the five core SEL competencies through second-grade language arts classes. For the self-awareness and social awareness competencies, lessons focus on naming emotion words, discussing the perspectives and emotions of characters in stories, and asking the children to share their favorite stories with explanations of why they like those stories (CASEL, 2020). Teacher practices that support those domains include practical feedback and encouragement of student reflection. Relationship skills and responsible decision-making competencies can be taught using stories that show decision-making and the resolution of conflict. Students can discuss the situations that characters faced and discuss how they responded and whether it was effective (CASEL, 2020).

Using Picture Books to Teach SEL in Elementary Grades

Children's books offer many lenses through which children can see themselves and others in the characters, plots, and themes. Books use stories, illustrations, and dialogue to show kindness and compassion, demonstrate problem-solving, display communication challenges, illustrate conflicts and their management and resolution, and present wise and poor decision-making. The use of books to teach, comfort, support, communicate, and build connections, with the goals of healing and personal growth, is referred to as *bibliotherapy* (McCullis, 2012).

Within the gifted setting, bibliotherapy has helped educators address a variety of social and emotional lessons and challenges, empowering children to develop healthy motivation and perfectionism, high self-esteem, strong communication and interpersonal relations, and a strong and healthy self-concept (Halsted, 2009; Lamont, 2012). Hébert, Long, and Neumeister (2000) describe the guided use of biographies in helping gifted young women develop resilience, establish healthy and supportive relationships, and understand gender role expectations.

Formal bibliotherapy involves a series of consecutive stages. The first is a reading, which is then followed by the child's identification and understanding of challenges, emotions, and responses within the text; their recognition and/or cathartic release of feelings; and a juxtaposition or linkage of the themes of the book with the child's issues or challenges, resulting in a sense of growth, healing, or resolution (Halsted, 2009; Hynes-Berry, 2012; Sullivan & Strang, 2002). Halsted (2009) describes a final stage, called universalization, the awareness that challenges are shared with many.

A lesson plan that uses bibliotherapy to teach SEL skills would typically have four components. The first is a group reading of the book and a reflection immediately afterwards that touches on the themes of the book and the actions and feelings of the characters, relating them back to how the children responded to the text. A second component is a group activity that reflects the lessons and values of the texts, such as discussions, role-playing, storytelling, art activities, or journaling and other writing activities (Hébert, 1997; Hynes-Berry, 2012). Reenactments of the stories in an informal setting, with improvisational lines and without formal props, immerses the students in the themes of the story, helping them to make connections among texts, to themselves, and with the global community. Other iterations of acting out the story include narrative pantomime, in which the whole group acts out the story as it is read by a narrator, and readers' theatre, a more formal presentation of the story that includes scripted lines and rehearsals (Hynes-Berry, 2012).

Retelling, reinterpretation, and reimagining of the stories—allowing children to tell stories in their own voice or through pictures—are also powerful iterations of bibliotherapy (Hynes-Berry, 2012). Writing original stories or poetry is also an effective exercise that can follow a story reading. In the exercise of "What Picture Do You See?," children are prompted to describe the images that come to mind after hearing a story; these pictures can be shared and discussed, with each student's image bringing to light a unique view of the story (Hynes-Berry, 2012).

The group reading and the group activity could be done in either order; in some cases a group activity that draws on the themes of the book is an effective way to start the lesson and lead into the reading. In other cases it is more effective to start with the reading and then follow it with a group activity that references the reading.

The third component of the bibliotherapy lesson plan is a differentiated learning stage that is customized for the ability levels and interests of the students. At the early elementary grades, this can include a choice board with such options as drawing a picture of the problem and solution; choosing four new words from the book and drawing a picture, using them in a sentence, or creating an acrostic poem with them; and describing the characters' emotions in words or pictures.

The fourth and final component of the bibliotherapy lesson is closure and reflection. This step can be done in the whole group, with students sorted into small groups, or as an individual reflection in which they share what they have learned. The students come together and share and discuss their findings.

Each lesson can teach individual SEL competencies or multiple domains, depending on the focus of the lesson, the age of the students, and the content used. For example, a lesson about conflict management would draw on recognizing and sharing emotions, making good decisions, and communicating clearly. The books can be subject-specific, focusing on such topics as language arts, social studies, and science.

In the next chapters, we will illustrate how to identify quality picture books and discuss the factors teachers need to take into consideration when choosing books for classroom or small-group settings, including children's interests and reading ability levels vs. content comprehension levels. The later chapters will consider how to address SEL in the specific content areas of science, social studies, and English-language arts (ELA).

References

American Psychological Association, Center for Psychology in Schools and Education. (2017). *Top 20 principles from psychology for preK-12 creative, talented, and gifted students' teaching and learning.* www.apa.org/ed/schools/teaching-learning/top-twenty-principles.aspx.

Ashdown, D. M., & Bernard, M. E. (2012). Can explicit instruction in social and emotional learning skills benefit the social-emotional development, well-being, and academic achievement of young children? *Early Childhood Education Journal, 39*(6), 397–405. https://doi.org/10.1007/s10643-011-0481-x

Berg, J., Osher, D., Same, M. R., Nolan, E., Benson, D., & Jacobs, N. (2017). *Identifying, defining, and measuring social and emotional competencies.* American Institutes for Research.

CASEL: History. (n.d.). CASEL. https://casel.org/history/
CASEL'S SEL framework: What are the core competence areas and where are they promoted? (2020). CASEL. www.casel.org/what-is-SEL
Clinkenbeard, P. R. (2012). Motivation and gifted students: Implications of theory and research. *Psychology in the Schools, 49*(7), 622–630.
Cohn, S. J. (2002). Gifted students who are gay, lesbian, or bisexual. In M. Neihart, S. M. Reis, N. M. Robinson, & S. M. Moon (Eds.), *The social and emotional development of gifted children: What do we know?* (pp. 145–153). Sourcebooks.
Colfer, E. (2001). *Artemis fowl.* Hyperion.
Conduct Problems Prevention Research Group. (2010). The effects of a multiyear universal social-emotional learning program: The role of student and school characteristics. *Journal of Consulting and Clinical Psychology, 78,* 156–168.
Cramer, K. M., & Castro-Olivo, S. (2016). Effects of a culturally adapted social-emotional learning intervention program on students' mental health. *Contemporary School Psychology, 20,* 118–129.
Dahl, R. (1988). *Matilda* (Q. Blake, Illus.). Jonathan Cape.
Daniels, S., & Piechowski, M. M. (2009). *Living with intensity: Understanding the sensitivity, excitability, and emotional development of gifted children, adolescents, and adults.* Great Potential Press, Inc.
Durlak, J. A., & Mahoney, J. L. (2019). *The practical benefits of an SEL program.* CASEL.
Dusenbury, L. et al. (2015). *What does evidence-based instruction in social and emotional learning actually look like in practice? Evidence-based instruction in social and emotional learning.* A Brief on Findings from CASEL's Program Reviews (pp. 1–6). CASEL. Retrieved from https://drc.casel.org/resources-by-topic/page/3/?topic=evidence-based-programs
Gagné, F. (2005a). From gifts to talents: The DMGT as a developmental model. In R. J. Sternberg & J. E. Davidson (Eds.), *Conceptions of giftedness* (2nd ed., pp. 98–120). Cambridge University Press.
Gagné, F. (2005b). From noncompetence to exceptional talent: Exploring the range of academic achievement within and between grade levels. *The Gifted Child Quarterly, 49*(2), 139–153. https://doi.org/10.1177/001698620504900204
Gross, C. M., Rinn, A. R., & Jamieson, K. M. (2007). Gifted adolescents' overexcitabilities and self-concepts: An analysis of gender and grade level. *Roeper Review, 29*(4), 240–248.

Halsted, J. W. (2009). *Some of my best friends are books: Guiding gifted readers from preschool to high school*. Great Potential Press, Inc.

Hamilton, L. S., & Doss, C. J. (2020). *Supports for social and emotional learning in schools: Findings from the American Teacher Panel*. RAND Corporation. www.rand.org/pubs/research_briefs/RBA397-1.html

Harrison, G. E., & Van Haneghan, J. P. (2011). The gifted and the shadow of the night: Dabrowski's overexcitabilities and their correlation to insomnia, death anxiety, and fear of the unknown. *Journal for the Education of the Gifted*, *34*(4), 669–697.

Hébert, T. P., & Furner, J. M. (1997). Helping high ability students overcome math anxiety through bibliotherapy. *Journal of Secondary Gifted Education*, *8*(4), 164–178.

Hébert, T. P., Long, L. A., & Neumeister, K. L. S. (2000). Using biography to counsel gifted young women. *Journal of Advanced Academics*, *12*(2), 62–79. https://doi.org/10.4219/jsge-2000-645

Hoffman, D. M. (2009). Reflecting on social emotional learning: A critical perspective on trends in the United States. *Review of Educational Research*, *79*(2), 533–556.

Hynes-Berry, M., & Chen, J.-Q. (2012). *Don't leave the story in the book: Using literature to guide inquiry in early childhood classrooms*. Teachers College Press.

Illinois State Board of Education. (n.d.). *Social/emotional learning standards*. www.isbe.net/Pages/Social-Emotional-Learning-Standards.aspx

Jinks, C. (2005). *Evil genius*. Harcourt.

Jones, S. M., & Bouffard, S. M. (2012). Social policy report: Social and emotional learning in schools from programs to strategies. *Sharing Child and Youth Development Knowledge*, *26*(4), 1–33.

Jones, S. M., et al. (2017). Promoting social and emotional competencies in elementary school. *The Future of Children*, *27*(1), 49–72.

Kane, M. (2009). Contemporary voices on Dabrowski's theory of positive disintegration. *Roeper Review*, *31*, 72–76.

L'Engle, M. (1962). *A wrinkle in time*. Ariel Books.

Lamont, R. T. (2012). The fears and anxieties of gifted learners: Tips for parents and educators. *Gifted Child Today Magazine*, *35*(4), 271–276. https://doi.org/10.1177/1076217512455479

Lieb, J. (2009). *I am a genius of unspeakable evil and I want to be your class president*. Razorbill.

Mahoney, J. L., Weissberg, R. P., Greenberg, M. T., Dusenbury, L., Jagers, R. J., Niemi, K., Schlinger, M., Schlund, J., Shriver, T. P., & VanAusdal, K. (2020). Systemic social and emotional learning: Promoting educational success for all preschool to high school students. *American Psychologist*. https://doi.org/10.1037/amp0000701.

Marsh, H. W., & Craven, R. G. (2000). Swimming in the school: Expanding the scope of the big fish little pond effect. In *Self-concept theory, research and practice: Advances for the new millennium* (p. 75). Proceedings of the inaugural international conference. University of Western Sydney.

Marsh, H. W., Trautwein, U., Lüdtke, O., Baumert, J., & Köller, O. (2007). The big-fish-little-pond effect: Persistent negative effects of selective high schools on self-concept after graduation. *American Educational Research Journal*, 44(3), 631–669.

McCoach, D. B., & Flake, J. K. (2018). The role of motivation. In S. I. Pfeiffer (Ed.), *APA handbook of giftedness and talent* (pp. 201–213). American Psychological Association.

McCulliss, D. (2012). Bibliotherapy: Historical and research perspectives. *Journal of Poetry Therapy*, 25(1), 23–38.

Mendaglio, S. (2012). Overexcitabilities and giftedness research: A call for a paradigm shift. *Journal for the Education of the Gifted*, 35(3), 207–219.

Moon, S. M. (2009). Myth 15: High-ability students don't face problems and challenges. *Gifted Child Quarterly* 53(4), 274–276.

NAGC. (n.d.-a). *Asynchronous development.* www.nagc.org/resources-publications/resources-parents/social-emotional-issues/asynchronous-development.

NAGC. (n.d.-b). *Gifted and LGBTQ+ advocacy.* www.nagc.org/get-involved/nagc-networks-and-special-interest-groups/special-interest-group-glbtq/glbtq-sig

Nathanson, L., Rivers, S. E., Flynn, L. M., & Brackett, M. A. (2016). Creating emotionally intelligent schools with RULER. *Emotion Review*, 8(4), 305–310.

Neihart, M. (1999). The impact of giftedness on psychological well-being: What does the empirical literature say? *Roeper Review*, 22(1), 10–17.

Neihart, M., & Yeo, L. S. (2018). Psychological issues unique to the gifted student. In S. I. Pfeiffer (Ed.), *APA handbook of giftedness and talent* (pp. 497–510). American Psychological Association.

Oberle, E., & Schonert-Reichl, K. A. (2017). *Social and emotional learning: Recent research and practical strategies for promoting children's social and emotional competence in schools* (pp. 175–197). Springer International Publishing. https://doi.org/10.1007/978-3-319-64592-6_11

Olszewski-Kubilius, P., & Calvert, E. (2015). Implications of the talent development framework for curriculum design. In *Modern curriculum for gifted and advanced academic student* (pp. 37–53). Prufrock Press.

Olszewski-Kubilius, P., Subotnik, R. F., & Worrell, F. C. (2018). *Talent development as a framework for gifted education: Implications for best practices and applications in schools*. Prufrock Press Inc.

Peters, S., & Engerrand, K. (2016). Equity and excellence: Proactive efforts in the identification of underrepresented students for gifted and talented services. *Gifted Child Quarterly, 60*(3), 159–171.

Preckel, F. et al. (2015). Gifted and maladjusted? Implicit attitudes and automatic associations related to gifted children. *American Educational Research Journal, 52*(6), 1160–1184

Reis, S. M., & Renzulli, J. S. (2004). Current research on the social and emotional development of gifted and talented students: Good news and future possibilities. *Psychology in the Schools, 41*(1), 119–130. https://doi.org/10.1002/pits.10144

Renzulli, J. S. (2005). The three-ring definition of giftedness: A developmental model for promoting creative productivity. In R. J. Sternberg & J. E. Davidson (Eds.), *Conceptions of giftedness* (2nd ed., pp. 246–280). Cambridge University Press.

Rice, K. G., & Taber, Z. B. (2018). Perfectionism. In S. I. Pfeiffer (Ed.), *Handbook of giftedness in children* (pp. 49–63). Springer.

Rinn, A. N. (2018). Social and emotional considerations for gifted students. In S. I. Pfeiffer (Ed.), *APA handbook of giftedness and talent* (pp. 453–464). American Psychological Association.

Rinn, A. N., & Majority, K. L. (2018). The social and emotional world of the gifted. In S. I. Pfeiffer (Ed.), *Handbook of giftedness in children* (pp. 49–63). Springer.

Robinson, N. M. (2002). *Assessing and advocating for gifted students: Perspectives for school and clinical psychologists*. Senior Scholars Series. https://eric.ed.gov/?id=ED476372

Schuler, P. (2002). *Perfectionism in gifted children and adolescents*. In M. Neihart, S. Reis, N. Robinson, & S. Moon (Eds.), The social and emotional development of gifted children. What do we know? (pp. 71–79). Prufrock Press.

Shechtman, Z., & Silektor, A. (2012). Social competencies and difficulties of gifted children compared to nongifted peers. *Roeper Review, 34,* 63–72.

Siegle, D., Gubbins, E., O'Rourke, P., Langley, S., Mun, R.O., Luria, S., et al. (2016). Barriers to underserved students' participation in gifted programs and possible solutions. *Journal for the Education of the Gifted, 39*(2), 103–131.

Silverman, L. K. (2000). The gifted individual. In L. K. Silverman (Ed.), *Counseling the gifted and talented* (pp. 3–28). Love Publishing.

Silverman, L. K. (2002). Asynchronous development. In M. Neihart, S. M. Reis, N. M. Robinson, & S. M. Moon (Eds.), *The social and emotional development of gifted children: What do we know?* (pp. 31–40). Sourcebooks.

Stewart, T. L. (2007). *The mysterious Benedict society.* Megan Tingley Books.

Subotnik, R. F., Olszewski-Kubilius, P., & Worrell, F. C. (2011). Rethinking giftedness and gifted education: A proposed direction forward based on psychological science. *Psychological Science in the Public Interest, 12*(1), 3–54. https://doi.org/10.1177/1529100611418056

Sullivan, A. K., & Strang, H. R. (2002). Bibliotherapy in the classroom using literature to promote the development of emotional intelligence. *Childhood Education, 79*(2), 74–80. https://doi.org/10.1080/00094056.2003.10522773

Taylor, R. D., Oberle, E., Durlak, J. A., & Weissberg, R. P. (2017). Promoting positive youth development through school-based social and emotional learning interventions: A meta-analysis of follow-up effects. *Child Development, 88*(4), 1156–1171.

Tillier, W. (2009). Dabrowski without the theory of positive disintegration just isn't Dabrowski. *Roeper Review, 31*(2), 123–126.

2

Choosing Quality Picture Books

Any educator who has had the powerful experience of connecting with a child through a beloved book knows the immeasurable value of a quality text. As educators, and mothers, we can each tell stories of the experiences we have had sharing books with children of all ages. Kathie, for example, shared *The Lorax* by Dr. Seuss with her elementary students every Earth Day and still enjoys sharing *Testing Miss Malarkey* by Judy Finchler every spring when standardized test pressures work their way into the lives of her teacher education students. As mothers, we both had the experience of reading *Guess How Much I Love You* by Sam McBratney and *Love You Forever* by Robert Munsch to our young children. Children, too, find joy in listening to or reading a story they have connected with, as any parent who has read the same book repeatedly at bedtime can confirm.

Educators who work with early elementary children know that "cracking the code" of early reading is a momentous occasion for a child, and many speak about the joy they feel when these young children embrace their new learning by devouring favorite books from the classroom or school library. As you read this chapter, you might think about books with which you have made powerful connections, perhaps books that you loved from your childhood or ones you have shared with your students or your own children. When these books come to mind, consider why you remember these books, sometimes many years later. As we discuss how to identify and choose quality picture books to support content area, literacy, and social and emotional learning (SEL), reflecting on the books that resonated with you and the reasons for these connections will help you frame your thinking about which books to make part of your teaching and why.

Chapter 1 provided a comprehensive overview of SEL. Building upon that foundation, this chapter considers how to choose the books that will best support integrating SEL within the teaching of the content areas and English Language Arts (ELA). First, we will explain how we are defining picture books, followed by a consideration of the unique qualities that make them particularly relevant for early elementary readers. Then, we will provide suggestions for how to identify quality picture books that deserve a prominent place in an educator's lessons and classroom library. Finally, we'll identify the ways that picture books can be of particular value as educators work to teach SEL within the content areas.

What Is a "Picture Book"?

Each of us probably has an image of our mind of what a picture book is. Picture books usually have limited text on the page, colorful images, fewer pages, and are physically larger than chapter books. These books tend to appeal to younger readers, although there are picture books with mature topics and themes, sophisticated vocabulary, and complex text structures that older readers can appreciate and enjoy. For purposes of this text, we borrow from the language of the Caldecott Medal, an award given to honor the artist of a distinguished children's picture book. We define a picture book as a book that provides a visual experience for the reader where the pictures provide support for the story, theme, or concept (American Library Association, 2021). These picture books are both literary and informational, including biography, and along with text, the pictures are essential to the story or presentation of information.

Picture books are unique because their two components, text and pictures, each play a major role. Unlike traditional children's chapter books where the pictures often contribute little to the overall story, in a picture book, both text and images are needed to fully comprehend the book's meaning. When considering the text, it is important to remember that these books are often designed to be read aloud. For this reason, all elements of the text must be considered: "Each syllable, each line break, each sentence's placement on the page and where those critical page-turns occur, the rhythm, the word choice, the repetition (and maybe even the rhyme, if it's done well)—all of these are massively important" (Johnston & Frazee, 2011, p. 10). Because these books are often very concise, each word must be considered for the value it contributes. In addition, because the illustrations are essential for comprehension, they are given as much consideration as the text. Wolfenberger and Sipe (2007), for example, note that any picture book can be considered a "sophisticated aesthetic object" (p. 279). Put another way, picture books combine text and illustrations into a whole that is greater than the sum of the parts.

The power of picture books is that "the words and pictures transact with each other, and transform each other" (Sipe, 1998, p. 98). A reader of a picture book uses the pictures to add meaning to the text, and the words to add meaning to the pictures. In some cases, the pictures and texts work together to tell the story (congruency), and in others the pictures are telling a different story (deviation) (Sipe, 1998). While congruency is most common, deviation can add depth, humor, and surprise to a picture book. For example, in the popular text *I Want My Hat Back* by Jon Klaussen, the bear asks the rabbit whether he has seen the bear's hat. The rabbit has the hat on his head, but he denies that he has seen it, and the bear continues on his search. This adds humor to the story, because the readers realize something the main character does not. In either case, deviation or congruency, the power of the picture book is in "the union of text and art that results in something beyond what each form separately contributes" (Wolfenbarger & Sipe, 2007, p. 273).

Another way to conceptualize the uniqueness of picture books is that the words and pictures rely upon different cognitive structures, those required for verbal information and those required for visual information (Sipe, 1998). Interestingly, in addition to contributing to the meaning of the book, these two different forms of information also influence how readers interact with a picture book. The verbal information encourages readers to read the text linearly and not interrupt the flow, whereas the illustrations encourage the reader to pause and look. This tension is powerful in picture books because it encourages rereading. The ideal picture book is one that allows children to have multiple experiences with it as they interact with words and text, and early elementary children can experience a picture book multiple times as they gain proficiency with the text and analyze the illustrations (Sipe, 1998).

The importance of this interplay between words and illustrations is reflected in the Common Core State Standards for English Language Arts. Anchor standard 7, which applies to both informational and literary texts, focuses on students' abilities to integrate and evaluate content presented in both words and images. This standard develops in complexity from asking kindergartners to be able to describe, with support, the relationship between the picture and the text to third graders being asked to articulate how the pictures contribute to the meaning of the text (National Governors Association Center for Best Practices and Council of Chief State School Officers, 2010). While the standard does not specify the use of picture books, they are ideal for addressing this standard because from their inception they are designed with the transaction between words and text at the forefront.

Why Use Picture Books?

There are numerous reasons to use picture books in an early elementary classroom, with readers of all ability levels. On a purely practical level, picture books are readily available through school and public libraries, as well as through digital platforms. They also cover a myriad of topics at a variety of different reading and content complexity levels. This is particularly important for differentiation because different books focused on a common topic or theme can meet the needs of readers at all levels of proficiency.

In an early elementary classroom, there will be a range of reading levels, and a benefit of a picture book is that even children in early stages of learning to read can begin to comprehend the book by looking at the pictures. With our youngest children, we use picture books because the pictures help tell the story. Before children learn to read, but after they have already acquired a sense of what a book "sounds like," they will flip through the pages of a new book, narrating a story as they do. As children get older and begin to learn to read independently, they will often shift to easier books that they can read independently, with assistance from the pictures; but read-alouds of high quality picture books will provide opportunities for exposure to and discussions on complex texts (Hoffman, Teale, & Yokota, 2015). This provides a depth to their reading lives beyond what they are capable of managing on their own. Conversely, more advanced readers may be able to manage the text independently or in a guided reading group. Some children, even strong readers, may not be comfortable transitioning to "chapter books," which are much longer and have fewer pictures. To expose children to more complex texts, an educator may use picture books of increasing difficulty. Picture books serve an invaluable purpose in literacy instruction even once most children in a classroom are reading proficiently. As children get older, educators continue to use picture books to create a shared experience, introduce new topics and ideas, and provide opportunities to discuss and analyze the interplay of text and visual images.

For educators who are looking for texts for their content area studies, picture books are particularly helpful. They can serve to create interest in a new topic by providing an introduction and serving as a starting place for further research. They also serve to give an in-depth look at a small piece of a particular topic or subject, especially important in subjects like science or social studies, where curricula are often criticized for being "an inch deep and a mile wide." This in-depth look also provides an opportunity to show a more human side of a subject, focusing on how one person was impacted by a specific historical event or how scientists overcame adversity as they worked to achieve their goals. Finally, picture books are brief, often only 32 or 48 pages long, and in

20 minutes an educator can provide an experience with a text that is both emotional and thought provoking (Pearson, 2005). Put another way, using picture books "in science, social studies, writing, and math instruction brings the topics under consideration to life and demonstrates how literature is a way of knowing the world in which we live, as well as an avenue of escape into other worlds" (Serafini, 2011, p. 32). Because picture books play an important role in a busy school day, identifying quality picture books is essential so that learning needs are met with books that are engaging and represent the diversity found in today's classrooms.

What Makes a Good Picture Book?

One of the most important considerations for choosing a picture book to use with a group of students is the educator's enthusiasm for the book (Weih, 2015). Being able to begin an activity by saying, "I have the greatest book to share with you today" will go far in encouraging students to engage fully with the lesson and the text. Of course, "greatest" can have many different meanings; a book can be the greatest because it is the funniest, or most interesting, or best matches the SEL, content, and ELA learning objectives. It is up to the educator to identify books that will appeal to the students while at the same time supporting the educational goals for the lesson or unit.

Initial Considerations

Before beginning our considerations for choosing picture books, we also want to note that while there are many, many good picture books on a variety of topics and themes, it will be rare that any one book will "check all of the boxes." For example, a book might address the content and SEL goals but be limited in its representation of diversity. Or, it might reflect diversity and address the SEL goals in a complete and appropriate way but not tie as closely to the content or learning standard as other books might. When this happens, it may be helpful to look at the totality of books presented within a unit or over the course of a year.

When a gap is identified, additional books can then be chosen to balance out the limitations, thus providing a comprehensive and inclusive text "diet" for the students.

From an educational perspective, sharing these sorts of considerations with children can be an important step in helping them develop early critical literacy skills. Children can be taught at a very young age to interrogate the texts by asking, for example, whose perspectives are here, and whose are missing? Who is visible in this book? Who are the authors, and what are their perspectives? Organizations such as We Need Diverse Books strive to make sure that all children can see themselves represented in the books they read, and they do this through advocating for changes in publishing, as well as working to support diverse publishing professionals, authors, and illustrators. This movement does not seek to prevent authors from writing about any topic they choose, but rather it focuses on centering authors who share the same characteristics (e.g., race, class, gender, language, dis/ability) as the individuals or characters in their books (Rodriguez, Gonzalez, & Rojas, 2020).

In addition to considering the authors' backgrounds, just as educators teach children to identify the connections they are making to a text (Harvey & Goudvis, 2017; Keene & Zimmerman, 2007), children can also be asked to make disconnections, pointing out when the lived experiences of the characters or individuals are significantly different from their own. The power in finding these disconnections is that students come to understand that "texts are constructed from a particular ideological standpoint, and therefore can be deconstructed, or questioned and critiqued" (Jones & Clarke, 2007, p. 104). For example, a viewing of the wordless picture book *The Midnight Fair* by Gideon Sterer could begin a powerful conversation. In this book, woodland creatures from a nearby forest enjoy the fair after all the humans have gone home for the night. At the same time children are engaged with the humorous illustrations that show weasels, bears, raccoons, and deer riding amusement rides, winning prizes, and enjoying snacks, they can share their own connections and disconnections with an experience at a fair.

When students are taught to think critically as they engage with the text, many books, regardless of their connections to students, can be used as powerful teaching tools. Some students may find that the books are similar to their lives; others may find them different. But everyone can develop their critical literacy skills by analyzing the ideologies presented in the text.

Similarly, not all books chosen need to be award winners or be among the best literature in order for them to be included in a classroom or home library. Carter (2010), for example, notes that much of what students will read will be "beloved mid-level books, not the junk and not the prizewinners" (p. 56). This puts the emphasis on finding books that students will want to read or listen to, so that they are able to grow as readers through frequent practice. However, given the limited time educators have to introduce books to their class, the process of choosing a text for a read aloud, or of giving it a central place in a specific lesson, should be a thoughtful one. There are two main areas of consideration when identifying the best books to use in the classroom: the overall quality of the texts and who is represented in the text.

Qualities of Literary and Informational Texts

Any quality picture book should have rich themes or central ideas, round characters or key individuals, complex illustrations, rich language, and an engaging, multi-layered plot (Hoffman, Teale, & Yokota, 2015). Themes or central ideas in a text generally need to be inferred through interaction with the text. For that reason, they require deep engagement, and readers may find that different themes are supported by evidence in the text. The characters or key individuals in the story should be dynamic and changing. Not only does this lead to a more interesting text, but it is these changes that support deep connections with SEL topics. Complex illustrations speak to the heart of picture books. As picture books are characterized by the interplay of text and image, complex illustrations contribute to the meaning conveyed by the text. The language of a picture book, just like the illustrations, has to be carefully constructed. These books are usually concise, so word choice is paramount. In succinct sentences, the author must convey meaning that is, at the same time, both complex and appropriate for younger readers. Finally, the plot or structure must be both complex and engaging. Young children are most often engaged by books that relate to their experiences. This is the reason why so many of the books that take on complex issues do so through the eyes of a child. When considering all of these elements of quality books, the focus should always be on what will keep the attention of the children who will read or listen to them (Weih, 2015). A book deemed to be "the best" by an adult will have little value if it does not engage its intended audience.

While these characteristics apply to both literary and informational texts, there are some considerations unique to informational texts. Gill (2009), for example, includes the characteristics described earlier but also reminds educators to choose books that are "accurate and authoritative" (p. 262). Because informational texts can be dense and readers may struggle to make meaning from them, particularly when the topic is unfamiliar, Weih (2015) focuses on characteristics that can engage readers and support their comprehension. He suggests that when choosing informational texts educators should begin with topics that would interest the students. From there, the next step should be to identify books that are creative, so they draw readers in with their uniqueness; have graphics that are clear, large, and attract the reader's attention; and have print that varies in size and style to both engage the reader and draw attention to key information or words. While informational texts often provide new challenges to readers, well-written texts engage readers by increasing their motivation through interesting topics, as well as by using text and graphic features to enhance their understanding.

Representation Matters

In addition to the overall quality of a picture book, an educator should also choose books that represent all of the different elements of diversity a child will encounter in a pluralist society. Picture books in the classroom should include diversity in race, culture, language, ability, gender/sex, and socio-economic status. Strykowski (2020), for example, notes that readers should "find characters to which they can connect—to feel included and be counted. Not only will children who read be entertained by first-hand adventures, but they will also gain new ways of thinking about and relating to those who may appear different from them" (p. 52). Put another way, when a classroom has books that are both mirrors, representing the lives of the children in that classroom, and windows, exposing children to a world different from their own, children learn to understand and appreciate the similarities and differences between all people (Bishop, 1990).

In addition, educators also want to make sure that they are looking for examples of representation that show both "average people" and heroes. For example, while it is beneficial for Black Indigenous People of Color (BIPOC) to see heroes or exemplary individuals who look like them, it is equally important for them to see children who have everyday experiences similar to their own (e.g., difficulties with parents or siblings, having fun with friends, trying out a new experience). This sort of representation is particularly important when addressing SEL. It may be difficult for children to identify a connection with someone who has achieved great success, but they more readily connect with a child from a similar background. Abellán-Pagnani and Hébert (2013), for example, provide the example of a teacher who used books with Latinx characters to "help her students understand themselves and cope with the challenges in their lives by providing them stories relevant to their personal situations and developmental needs as young children" (p. 50). In addition to the everyday experiences, picture book biographies can also play an important role in developing the self-concept of all students, but they may be imperative for BIPOC students who may not see role models who look like them celebrated frequently. These books can serve to inspire and motivate students as they study individuals who overcame hardships to attain success in a particular field (Abellán-Pagnani & Hébert, 2013; Floyd & Hébert, 2010).

Picture books also serve as an important window on society. Children who are able to interact with characters or individuals who are different from them in some way, but also have a set of similar experiences, are more likely to understand or empathize with people from that background. A search of publications on the use of picture books in classrooms shows that many authors assert that books about people of color (e.g., Gaston, 2020), members of the LGBTQIA community (e.g., Casciola, 2013; Sciurba, 2017; Young, 2019), individuals with disabilities (e.g., Pennell, Wollak, & Koppenhaver, 2018), religious minorities (e.g., Baer, 2017), those being raised in poverty (e.g., Quast & Bazemore-Bertrand, 2019), and those whose first language is not English (Koss & Daniel, 2018) serve a dual purpose in the classroom. They allow children who identify as a member of one or more of these groups to enhance their self-esteem by seeing themselves represented in books, and children who are not members of these groups learn to empathize by seeing that these children experience many of the challenges and emotions they do.

All of these various considerations for choosing quality picture books can be somewhat overwhelming. Fortunately, there are numerous lists and guidelines available to assist educators wanting to find quality picture books for use with children (see Table 2.1). In addition, many states have their own awards. In our home state of Illinois, the Monarch Awards (run by the Association of Illinois School Library Educators) allow children and educators to nominate books appealing to children in grades K-3.

Table 2.1 Resources for Finding Quality Picture Books

Award Winners (American Library Association)

Caldecott Medal • For the most distinguished American picture book for children • www.ala.org/alsc/awardsgrants/bookmedia/caldecott	*Robert F. Sibert Informational Book Medal* • For the most distinguished informational book published in the United States in English • www.ala.org/alsc/awardsgrants/bookmedia/sibert
Belpré Award • For a Latino/Latina writer and illustrator whose work best portrays, affirms, and celebrates the Latino cultural experience • http://www.ala.org/alsc/awardsgrants/bookmedia/belpre	*Geisel Award* • Most distinguished American book for beginning readers • www.ala.org/alsc/awardsgrants/bookmedia/geisel

Choosing Quality Picture Books ♦ 41

Award Winners (American Library Association)

Coretta Scott King Award
- For outstanding African American authors and illustrators of books who demonstrate an appreciation of African American culture and universal human values
- www.ala.org/rt/emiert/cskbookawards

Asian/Pacific American Award
- Honors individual work about Asian/Pacific Americans and their heritage
- www.apalaweb.org/awards/literature-awards/

Schneider Family Book Award
- Presented to an author or illustrator for a book that embodies an artistic expression of the disability experience
- www.ala.org/awardsgrants/schneider-family-book-award

Rainbow Book List
- An annual annotated bibliography consisting of quality LGBTQIA+ literature
- www.ala.org/awardsgrants/rainbow-project-book-list

Stonewall Book Awards
- Presented to English language books that have exceptional merit relating to the LGBTQIA+ experience.
- www.ala.org/rt/rrt/award/stonewall/honored

Journals, Magazines, and Newspapers With Online Reviews

The Horn Book
www.hbook.com

Booklist
www.booklistonline.com

School Library Journal
www.slj.com

Kirkus Reviews
www.kirkusreviews.com

Publishers Weekly
www.publishersweekly.com

The New York Times
www.nytimes.com/column/childrens-books

Social Media Sites

Social Justice Book Lists
- More than 80 carefully selected lists of multicultural and social justice books
- https://socialjusticebooks.org/booklists

Children's Literature Portraying Religious Diversity in the US
- Lists of quality books that focus on authentic expressions of religious diversity for children grades K-4
- https://lib.stpetersburg.usf.edu/ChildrensLiteratureReligiousDiversity

(Continued)

Table 2.1 (Continued)

Social Media Sites	
Goodreads • A site that creates lists based on readers' reviews. • www.goodreads.com/	*We Need Diverse Books* • Advocacy organization that promotes changes in the publishing industry to promote and produce diverse children's literature • Gives out the Walter Award for diverse authors of books for ages 9–13 and teens. • www.diversebooks.org/

Other Resources	
Bank Street Best Children's Books of the Year • Annual publication by the Children's Book Committee that aims to guide educators, librarians, and caregivers to the best children's books published each year • www.bankstreet.edu/library/center-for-childrens-literature/childrens-book-committee/best-childrens-books-of-the-year	*Orbis Pictus Award* • Awarded by the National Council of Teachers of English for excellence in the writing of nonfiction for children • www.ncte.org/awards/orbis-pictus-award-nonfiction-for-children

The children then have the opportunity to read the books and vote on their favorite one. While the books on this list are not limited to picture books, given the early elementary grade range, many are. A search for similar awards in your state may point you to picture books that young children in your state have identified as good, as well as provide an opportunity to get students involved in thinking about the characteristics of an award-winning book.

How Do We Connect Picture Books to Social and Emotional Learning?

As discussed previously, quality children's books provide a powerful base from which to begin integrating SEL with teaching in the content areas and ELA. In their article on using children's books to teach SEL, Heath, Smith, and Young

(2017) call this connection a "natural extension of teachers' existing skills" (p. 551), and in considering book choices, it is helpful to think of SEL integration as an extension of the content area and literacy learning. While considerations will be different for each area, as you review picture books for use within a particular content area or literacy focus, you can also view them through an SEL lens, looking for relevance to the Collaborative for Academic, Social, and Emotional Learning (CASEL) competencies (i.e., self-awareness, self-management, social awareness, relationship skills, or responsible decision-making), Harvard SEL domains (i.e., emotion, cognitive, social, values, perspectives, identity), and/or connections to your specific SEL curriculum.

Teaching Considerations

A review of the Common Core State Standards and other national standards documents provides additional support for the goal of integrating SEL with learning in ELA and the content areas. For example, the Common Core standards document points out that students who have met the standards will "come to understand other perspectives and cultures" (NGACBP & CCSSO, 2010, p. 7). This clear connection shows that as students interact with texts through reading, writing, listening, and speaking, they will be exposed to ideas and experiences that are outside of their own lives. This assists with the development of empathy and supports critical thinking skills that will be essential throughout their lives, as children can use these diverse perspectives to consider alternate points of view. In the C3 Social Studies framework document, the introductory materials note that students must be "aware of their changing cultural and physical environments" and "act in ways that promote the common good" (National Council for the Social Studies, 2013, p. 5). As with the Common Core, it is clear that the cognitive, social, and emotional components of SEL can be addressed in unison with the content area standards.

In choosing books, it is essential that teachers are aware of the lived experiences of their students. While it is important to expose children to the experiences of others, educators should be alert to situations where, in the process of increasing empathy and compassion in one group of children (often those from majority cultures), other children are made to feel uncomfortable or are perhaps traumatized (Katch, 2018). If this were to be a concern, a conversation with the parents, or, perhaps, the children themselves would be appropriate. For example, while a book like *Milo Imagines the World* by Matt de la Peña shares a powerful message about not judging people by their outward experience, Milo, his older sister, and his grandmother are taking a long bus ride to visit his mother in jail. For a child who has taken a similar trip to visit a loved one, this book may make an already difficult set of experiences more challenging. It is also important to note that children should be encouraged to have ownership over their own life stories. They do not have to share, and they should not ever be responsible for speaking for an entire group of people.

Finally, diverse picture books can be important for both the learning of the teacher and the students. Teachers from a majority culture may find themselves expanding their understanding of the backgrounds and cultural capital of the children in their classroom through books that represent diverse ethnicities, cultures, languages, etc. More importantly, students benefit from "culturally relevant" teaching practices. It is well established that when students have a healthy self-concept and pride in their cultural identity, their academic success will increase. Gloria Ladson-Bilings (1995), who introduced the term *culturally relevant pedagogy*, noted: "Culturally relevant teachers utilize students' culture as a vehicle for learning" (p. 161). She provided several examples from her research of the positive effect this had on students' academic success. By making thoughtful book choices, teachers can increase their knowledge and have a positive influence on both the students' self-concept and their academic achievement.

References

Abellán-Pagnani, L., & Hébert, T. P. (2013). Using picture books to guide and inspire young gifted Hispanic students. *Gifted Child Today*, *36*(1), 47–56. https://doi.org/10.1177/1076217512459735

Baer, A. L. (2017). Beyond the veil: Exploring Muslim cultures through children's picture books. *Ohio Journal of English Language Arts*, *57*(1), 23–29.

Bishop, R. S. (1990). Mirrors, windows, and sliding glass doors. *Perspectives: Choosing and Using Books for the Classroom*, *6*(3), ix–xi.

American Library Association. (2021, March 24). Randolph Caldecott Medal. *American Library Association*. https://www.ala.org/alsc/awardsgrants/bookmedia/caldecott

Carter, B. (2010, July/August). Not the Newbury: Books that make the reader. *The Horn Book Magazine*, *86*(4), 52–56.

Casciola, V. (2013). Creating a space for all children: Providing LGBTQ literature in the classroom. *Journal of Reading Education*, *39*(1), 34–35.

Floyd, E. F., & Hébert, T. P. (2010). Using picture book biographies. *Gifted Child Today*, *33*(2), 38–46.

Gaston, S. (2020). The necessity of seeing positive Black characters. *Literacy Today*, *38*(2), 58–58.

Gill, S. R. (2009). What teachers need to know about the "new" nonfiction. *The Reading Teacher*, *63*(4), 260–267. https://doi.org/10.1598/RT.63.4.1

Harvey, S., & Goudvis, A. (2017). *Strategies that work: Teaching comprehension to enhance understanding* (3rd ed.). Stenhouse.

Heath, M., Smith, K., & Young, E. (2017). Using children's literature to strengthen social and emotional learning. *School Psychology International*, *38*(5), 541–561. https://doi.org/10.1177/0143034317710070

Hoffman, J. L., Teale, W. H., & Yokota, J. (2015). The book matters! Choosing complex narrative texts to support literacy discussions. *Young Children*, *70*(4), 8–15.

Johnston, A., & Frazee, M. (2011). Why we're still in love with picture books (even though they're supposed to be dead). *Horn Book Magazine*, *87*(3), 10–16.

Jones, S., & Clarke, L. W. (2007). Disconnections: Pushing readers beyond connections and toward the critical. *Pedagogies: An International Journal*, *2*(2), 95–115. https://doi.org/10.1080/15544800701484069

Katch, J. (2018). Seeing me in you: Teaching empathy and learning courage through picture books. *Schools: Studies in Education*, *15*(2), 216–227.

Keene, E., & Zimmerman, S. (2007). *Mosaic of thought: The power of comprehension strategy instruction* (2nd ed.). Heinemann.

Koss, M. D., & Daniel, M. C. (2018). Valuing the lives and experiences of English Learners: Widening the landscape of children's literature. *TESOL Journal, 9*, 431–454. https://doi.org/10.1002/tesj.336

Ladson-Bilings, G. (1995). But that's just good teaching! The case for culturally relevant pedagogy. *Theory into Practice, 34*(3), 159–165.

National Council for the Social Studies. (2013). *The college, career, and civic life (C3) framework for social studies state standards: Guidance for enhancing the rigor of K-12 civics, economics, geography, and history.* National Council for the Social Studies (NCSS).

National Governors Association Center for Best Practices, Council of Chief State School. (2010). *Common core state standards: English language arts.* National Governors Association Center for Best Practices, Council of Chief State School Officers. www.corestandards.org/wp-content/uploads/ELA_Standards.pdf.

Pearson, M. B. (2005). Speaking to their hearts: Using picture books in the history classroom. *Library Media Collection, 24*(3), 30–32.

Pennell, A. E., Wollak, B., & Koppenhaver, D. A. (2018). Respectful representations of disability in picture books. *The Reading Teacher, 71*(4), 411–419.

Quast, E., & Bazemore-Bertrand, S. (2019). Exploring economic diversity and inequity through picture books. *The Reading Teacher, 73*(2), 219–222. https://doi.org/10.1002/trtr.1807

Rodriguez, S. C., Gonzalez, K., & Rojas, C. (2020). Immigration picture books by #ownvoices authors. *Georgia Journal of Literacy, 43*(2), Article 5. Retrieved February 15, 2021, from https://digitalcommons.kennesaw.edu/gjl/vol43/iss2/5

Sciurba, K. (2017). Flowers, dancing, dresses, and dolls: Picture book representations of gender-variant males. *Children's Literature in Education, 48*(3), 276–293.

Serafini, F. (2011). Creating space for children's literature. *The Reading Teacher, 65*(1), 30–34 https://doi.org/10.1598/RT.65.1.4

Sipe, L. R. (1998). How children's books work: A semiotically frame theory of text-picture relationships. *Children's Literature in Education, 29*(2), 97–108.

Strykowski, M. (2020). Choosing books for today's children. *Knowledge Quest, 48*(4), 50–52.

Weih, T. G. (2015). *How to select books for teaching to children: Taking a critical look at books through a pedagogical lens.* University of Northern Iowa. https://files.eric.ed.gov/fulltext/ED554313.pdf

Wolfenberger, C. D., & Sipe, L. R. (2007). A unique visual and literary art form: Recent research on picture books. *Language Arts*, *84*(3), 273–280.

Young, C. A. (2019). Interrogating the lack of diversity in award-winning LGBTQ-inclusive picturebooks. *Theory Into Practice*, *58*(1), 61–70.

Book List

De La Peña, M. (2021). *Milo imagines the world* (C. Robinson, Illus.). G.P. Putnam's Sons Books for Young Readers.

Finchler, J. (2003). *Testing Miss Malarkey* (K. O'Malley, Illus.). Bloomsbury.

Jeffers, O., & Winston, S. (2016). *A child of books* (O. Jeffers & S. Winston, Illus.). Candlewick.

Klaussen, J. (2011). *I want my hat back* (J. Klaussen, Illus.). Candlewick.

McBratney, S. (2019). *Guess how much I love you* (A. Jeram, Illus.). Candlewick.

Munsch, R. (1995). *Love you forever* (S. McGraw, Illus.). Firefly Books.

Seuss, Dr. (1990). *The lorax* (Dr. Seuss, Illus.). Random House Books for Young Readers.

Sterer, G. (2021). *The midnight fair* (M. Di Giorgio, Illus.). Candlewick.

3

Matching Children to Books

Choosing a book for a whole group lesson, small group work, or a child's individual reading can be a little like finding a perfect gift. Taking into account everything you know about the intended receiver, you strive for a perfect match. However, you are limited by constraints, including availability and your own budget. As an educator, an ideal book match for a child only comes after reflection on key questions such as: What content and/or standards does this book need to support? What are the reading challenges and strengths of the children who will read or listen to the book? What is the task that students will complete based on the book? What are the interests of the readers? What are the identities of the children who will read the book? Like gift giving, a "perfect" match is rare, but reflecting on these questions as part of the lesson-planning process will more likely mean that the books in the hands of the children meet the needs of the lesson and the individual learners.

Before delving into the specifics of how to match children to books, there are two main principles that underlie the specific considerations outlined in this chapter. First, while there are some minor areas of disagreement among researchers within the field of literacy education, it is widely accepted that students will grow as readers when they read books that provide plenty of opportunity for success but also small challenges (Allington, McCuiston, & Billen, 2015) in areas such as vocabulary, text structures, and genre. Second, researchers also distinguish

DOI: 10.4324/9781003247425-4

between text complexity and text difficulty; *text complexity* refers to characteristics of the text in isolation, while *text difficulty* considers the interaction between the reader and text (Amendum, Conradi, & Hieber, 2018; Sierschynsk, Louie, & Pughe, 2014). In other words, the complexity of a text will not differ depending on whose hands it is in, while text difficulty will. For example, given two readers at approximately the same reading level, one may find a book "easy" because they have vast experience with the content, while another, without similar background knowledge, may find the same book "difficult."

Chapter 2 delineated the characteristics of quality picture books, including carefully crafted texts and complex illustrations, as well as authors and characters that represent all of the areas of diversity found in classrooms and society as a whole. This chapter builds on these themes and adds an additional layer by considering the unique needs of the individual students. As you read this chapter, it is important to remember that this matching process, like much about educating children, can be seen as both an "art" and a "science." Kathie's students, future elementary educators, will often approach her to ask if a book is "right" for a particular grade level or lesson, and her response is often a very unsatisfying version of "It depends." This chapter provides an overview of three factors on which a good match "depends." When considering text complexity, an educator should consider quantitative measures, qualitative measures, and reader/task factors.

Quantitative Measures

While any system of identifying a "best fit" book for a child has its limitations, for many educators, the initial process of matching children and texts begins with an assessment of a student's reading level and a quantitative measure of text complexity. Using a planned assessment process, students will be assigned a reading level (e.g., Lexile, Guided Reading, Accelerated Reader) and, using various online tools such as Scholastic's "Book Wizard" or Lexile's "Find a Book," an educator can search for a level by a book title or find books within a given reading level range. In addition, when a text is not in an existing database on the Lexile website, an educator can also upload a portion of a text for analysis and leveling. While it may be tempting to end the process of matching a book to a child here, this should only be the first step. An understanding of how quantitative measures work will help illustrate why a match between a child's assessed reading level and a book's measured complexity level should only be an initial step in finding a "best-fit" book.

While there are numerous quantitative scales for determining a text's complexity, one of the more frequently used is Lexile Measures. A quantitative scale such as this uses an algorithm that considers text factors such as sentence length and word frequency to determine a level for a text. The Lexile Framework suggests that the "sweet spot" for readers is from 100 below their current level to 50 above their level (MetaMetrics, 2020). In other words, based on this scale, a second grader who is evaluated to be reading at a 450 Lexile level should be given texts between 350 and 500. However, even within this set of quantitative measures it is clear that a purely quantitative system of measuring text complexity does not encompass all of the unique and diverse characteristics of the texts children read.

To address the factors that go beyond the quantitative measures, the Lexile system includes a series of codes that provide some qualitative guidance for matching children to books and illustrate the limitations of any quantitative leveling system. For example, a search for picture books by Lexile levels will result in a list with many texts coded with an "AD" for "adult directed" before the Lexile number. This means that the book is best read aloud, with adult guidance. Many classic and contemporary picture books, such as *Where the Wild Things Are* (AD 740L) by Maurice Sendak and *Fireboat: The Heroic Adventures of the John J. Harvey* (AD 600L) by Maira Kalman have quantitative Lexile measures that place them at a second- or third-grade reading level, but the complexity of topics and themes makes adult guidance an important component when sharing the book with children. *Where the Wild Things Are* deals with a child's inability to control his rage. He is sent to his room without supper, but through his fantasy world he finds an outlet for his anger, before returning to his room where his dinner has been left for him and is still warm. A more recent example of a similarly "easy" picture book with complex themes is *Fireboat: The Heroic Adventures of the John J. Harvey*, which tells the story of a New York City retired fireboat called into action on September 11, 2001 to help douse the flames at the World Trade Center site. In both cases, these are books that quantitatively might be a good "match" for early elementary students, but the strong emotions evoked would suggest adult guidance to make them appropriate for seven- or eight-year-olds.

The Lexile measurement system also moves beyond an initial quantitative measurement by providing two other codes that can be of assistance to educators endeavoring to find books on a common topic or theme that meets the needs of a wide range of learners. In addition to the numeric value, some books are labeled NC for "non-conforming" and HL for "high-low." A non-conforming book is one that has a higher reading level but is still appropriate for younger readers. For gifted readers, a "non-conforming" book like *The Storm Book* by Charlotte Zaltow, a Caldecott Honor Book from 1989, has a Lexile level of 1030 but is only 32 pages and, while the pages have extensive text, each page has a picture that helps support a reader's understanding of the story. Conversely, a "high-low" book is a one with a lower Lexile measure but content that would be appropriate for older readers. Most of these books are chapter books with topics appropriate for older readers but at reading levels in the second- to fourth-grade range.

Finally, quantitative measures need to be considered carefully in the early elementary grades. Research has shown that they are much less effective before second grade because "texts for kindergarten and grade 1 . . . often contain difficult-to-assess features designed to aid early readers in acquiring written language" (National Governors Association Center for Best Practices & Council of Chief State School Officers, 2010). Even within a quantitative system like the Lexile Measures, these nuances, including times where the level of content and complexity of the text do not align, and the unique difficulties with leveling early elementary texts, make it clear that additional analysis must be undertaken when matching children with books. While a traditional method for leveling texts may ask educators to begin with one or more quantitative measures before using qualitative measures to move a text up or down as needed, in the early elementary grades, educators may need to focus more on the qualitative and reader/task factors as they identify which books to use with the children in their classrooms.

Qualitative Measures

Qualitative measures, or those that are distinguished based on the judgements of a human reader, are powerful for two reasons. First, they can help provide a level of nuance in the process of matching children with books that is not possible with quantitative measures. Second, the process of analysis may provide educators with insights into the text that can assist them as they plan lessons for students. As noted previously, there are many times when the quantitative measures of text complexity are not enough. A book may have simple words and sentence structures, but the topics or themes may be too complex for young children to manage independently. Or, a simpler topic may be addressed with figurative language or less familiar structures, once again adding an additional level of complexity.

When looking at qualitative measures of text complexity, there are four main areas for consideration. These are: levels of meaning or purpose, structure, language conventionality and clarity, and knowledge demands. Table 3.1 provides suggestions for questions a text reviewer can ask in order to determine the complexity of the text. While there are some differences between how complexity is defined for literary and informational texts, the types of questions asked are similar.

Within the category of structure, it is important to consider the important role that graphics play in books for the youngest readers. As a general rule, books with graphics that are simple and carry little of the meaning tend to be simpler than books with graphics that need to be interpreted or analyzed in order

Table 3.1 Questions for Considering Text Complexity Using Qualitative Factors

Qualitative Factor	Questions to Ask
Levels of Meaning or Purpose	• Is there one level of meaning, or are there multiple levels of meaning? (literary text) • Is the purpose explicitly stated, or must it be inferred? (informational text)
Structure	• Is the organization simple or complex, and are connections explicit or implicit? • Is the structure conventional or unconventional? • Are events presented chronologically/logically, or are there jumps in time or flashbacks? • Are the traits common to a genre or a unique disciplinary structure? (especially informational text) • Are the graphics simple or complex? • Are the graphics relevant and supportive of the readers' meaning making?
Language Conventionality and Clarity	• Is the language primarily literal or figurative/ironic? • Is the language clear or ambiguous/purposefully misleading? • Is the language contemporary or familiar, or archaic or otherwise unfamiliar? • Is the language conversational, or does the text contain numerous general academic or domain-specific words?
Knowledge Demands: Life Experiences (literary texts)	• Is the theme simple or complex/sophisticated? • Is there a single theme, or are there multiple themes? • Are the experiences common, everyday experiences or clearly fantastical situations? Are the experiences distinctly different from the reader's own? • Is there a single perspective, or are there multiple perspectives? • Are the perspectives similar to the reader's, or are they unlike or in opposition to the reader's perspective?
Knowledge Demands: Cultural/Literary Knowledge (chiefly literary texts)	• Does comprehension require everyday knowledge and familiarity with common genre conventions, or is additional cultural and literary knowledge useful? • Are there few references or allusions to other texts (low intertextuality), or are there many references/allusions (high intertextuality)?
Knowledge Demands: Content/Discipline Knowledge (chiefly informational texts)	• Does comprehension require everyday knowledge and familiarity with common genre conventions, or is extensive content knowledge required? • Are there few references to/citations of other texts (low intertextuality), or are there many references to/citations of other texts (high intertextuality)?

Source: Adapted from: *Common Core State Standards for English language arts and literacy in history/social studies, science, and technical subjects: Appendix A: Research supporting key elements of the standards and glossary of key terms.*

to fully understand the meaning. However, in books for the earliest readers, the graphics often play an important role in supporting meaning-making. For this reason, as educators are analyzing the qualitative features of a book, they will need to pay particular attention to the role of the graphics (National Governors Association Center for Best Practices & Council of Chief State School Officers, 2010). Books that have congruency between images and text (i.e., they tell the same story) will be more supportive of readers than books that have deviation between images and text (i.e., they are communicating different messages).

Reader and Task Factors

In addition to the numerous considerations for assessing the complexity of a text qualitatively and quantitatively, there are also many factors external to the text that will influence how a teacher matches books to children. While it is common for educators to begin with quantitative factors, and then use qualitative factors to shift a book up or down within a grade band, some researchers assert that reader and task factors should be considered early on in the analysis process. For example, Wixson and Valencia (2014) state: "We suggest that reader and task factors be among the first considerations in measuring text complexity because they are likely to be the most important factors in determining the comprehension of complex text in a specific instructional context" (p. 431). They remind educators that complexity is not a factor residing in the text. Instead, it exists only when text, reader, and task are considered together. Readers bring much to the table as they begin to interact with their books.

Consider, for example, any group of early elementary children you know. Before you read this section, brainstorm everything you know about those children as readers. Odds are you will have identified characteristics such as their attention span, whether or not they are able to draw inferences, whether or not they are confident readers, and perhaps something about their interests, background knowledge, or first language. These descriptors get at the heart of the reader factors that play an important role in how educators match children to books. The RAND Reading Study Group (2002) included these descriptors within the categories of cognitive capacities, motivation, and types of knowledge, and these characteristics play an important role in what a "just right" book is for an individual child.

Readers who understand their purpose for reading, are interested in the content, and have a strong self-efficacy (RAND, 2002) are likely to be more willing to persevere through a challenging text than students who are confused by the purpose or unmotivated by reading for school, indifferent to the topic, or unsure of their reading abilities. Thinking about readers you know, you may have seen a child read books in the Harry Potter series in order to share in the enthusiasm for the books shown by older siblings, or sports-loving children read articles in the newspaper, or online, significantly above their reading level because they want to understand the latest news about a favorite athlete or team. Similarly, a student who has a lot of knowledge about the general vocabulary used, the vocabulary specific to the topic, or a familiarity with the genre or style of writing may be able to successfully read and enjoy texts at a higher reading level. All of these considerations are "reader factors" that should be given as much consideration when matching children and books as quantitative and qualitative measures.

In addition to factors specific to the reader, there are also three areas to consider when determining how the task will influence how a book is matched with a child. These are: the amount of support the child will be given as they are reading, the complexity of the activity they are being asked to complete, and the intended consequence of the reading (Wixson & Valencia, 2014). As you consider these components, you might think about a book you read in middle school or high school that did not feel like a good fit, even if you were a proficient reader. Perhaps it was *Romeo and Juliet* by William Shakespeare or *A Christmas Carol* by Charles Dickens. For most readers, these books were perceived as challenging, and comprehension required guidance from the teacher (or perhaps the purchase of Cliffs Notes or SparkNotes from the local bookstore). In most instances, during your first read-through of the text, you likely focused primarily on trying to understand the plot, with deeper connections and analysis left for a later date.

As noted earlier, considering whether a text is to be read aloud with students or read by a child independently is an important factor in determining whether a book is an appropriate match for a reader. Just as the Lexile measures denote some texts as "Adult Directed," educators should consider their role in the reading process. The educator's level of facilitation of the comprehension process greatly influences students' abilities to manage the text (Valencia, Wixson, & Pearson, 2014). As part of a whole-group or small-group lesson, an educator can provide definitions of key vocabulary or give background or context to support comprehension. At the same time, the educator is likely also observing the students for signs of confusion, listening in as students are encouraged to "turn and talk" with a partner about a key plot point, and pausing to ask questions to determine whether students are comprehending. All of these typical teaching moves will provide a level of support that will make a more challenging text accessible to students.

While the focus is often on the level of challenge presented by the text, the assigned task also plays an important role. Wixson and Valencia (2014) note that an educator can "'change the difficulty of a text and students' ability to deeply comprehend and learn by altering the task" (p. 432). A teacher introducing a complex text might, on day one, for example, only expect that students will listen to the text and perhaps engage in a whole-group conversation or a partner discussion. This "task" asks students to demonstrate basic understanding, but nothing more. Contrast this with a task where students are asked to listen to a story read aloud before writing or drawing what they thought the key message or theme of the story was. While in both instances, the text was the same, the complexity of the task impacted the perceived complexity.

Readers read for different purposes, and these purposes influence the appropriateness of the texts they are reading. Generally these purposes can be grouped into three main categories: knowledge, application, and engagement (RAND, 2002). In a classroom, a teacher may ask: Is a child reading to learn something, to apply knowledge to something, or to engage with the text? Consider the different types of reading you do within a day. You may read a biography of a famous person or a magazine article on a science topic because you are interested and would like to know more (knowledge). You may read an instruction manual or a cookbook in order to learn how to work a new appliance or prepare a recipe (application). You may pick up the latest novel by a favorite author to read by the pool on your summer vacation (engagement). Children, even at a young age, will read for similar purposes, and these purposes should be taken into account when finding books. Texts read purely for enjoyment are usually more motivating, so students may be able to persevere through more challenging texts. Texts read for application or knowledge, especially on unfamiliar topics, may be perceived to be more challenging because of the different purpose and the lack of background knowledge. For that reason, a simpler book may be a better match than a more complex one.

Gifted Readers' Unique Needs

In addition to the broad consideration of quantitative measures, qualitative measures, and reader/task factors, there are also unique challenges to consider when working with gifted readers. First, the repetition and isolation of skills that may be necessary for some typically developing students may not be necessary for gifted early elementary students. Commenting on the literacy development of gifted learners in Italian preschools, Beltchenko (2020) notes: "Stringent and rigid curriculum is not in the best interest of the young child, especially for a young child who has the potential to think and perform above his or her age peers" (p. 79). Specifically the author advocates for the use of inquiry, books, and the child's own curiosity to guide the learning process. In addition, the Common Core State Standards, when suggesting appropriate level texts for each grade band, note that the unique needs of gifted or stronger readers must be considered in the process of matching children to books: "Students for whom texts within their text complexity grade band (or even from the next higher band) present insufficient challenge must be given the attention and resources necessary to develop their reading ability at an appropriately advanced pace" (NGACBP & CCSSO, 2010, p. 9). While the standards documents may place an emphasis on choosing books from higher grade bands, there are other ways to meet the unique needs of gifted readers.

One area for educators to consider is the totality of a student's reading and how it complements the teacher's instruction. Mesmer, Cunningham, and Hiebert (2012) write about a "diet of texts" and note that a reader's diet "provides and limits their opportunities to benefit from points of overlap between text complexity and reading instruction" (p. 247). Ideally, a reader should have opportunities in the text they read to both reinforce the teacher's instruction, but also self-teach as they work through complex texts at their reading level. Gifted readers may be more empowered to self-teach when reading because they are approaching a text with a strong set of reading skills (Connor et al., 2009). For that reason, educators should pay particular attention to the "diet" of these readers. In addition to increasing the level of difficulty, educators can help support students' reading growth and self-teaching by providing longer texts to build stamina, as well as by considering the multiple qualitative measures of text complexity. Books with unique structures, multiple purposes, new information, etc., can all provide a needed challenge for a gifted reader.

This match between book and reader is essential to students' literacy growth because when students are matched to books that provide appropriate challenge and introductions to new content, students are supporting existing reading skills, developing new ones, and learning content that supports them as they encounter new texts and challenges. The RAND Corporation (2002), for example, states: "As a reader begins to read and completes whatever activity is at hand, some of the knowledge and capabilities of the reader change" (p. 13). This makes the process particularly challenging because the "best fit" book for a child is a target that is always moving. The child is learning and growing with each book, and even as they are reading. However, an educator who is knowledgeable about the interplay of quantitative, qualitative, and reader/task factors in understanding text complexity will also be more adept at matching children to books and, where necessary, identifying mismatches and making the needed changes.

References

Allington, R. L., McCuiston, K., & Billen, M. (2015). What Research says about text complexity and learning to read. *Reading Teacher, 68*(7), 491–501.

Amendum, S. J., Conradi, K., & Hieber, E. (2018). Does text complexity matter in the elementary grades? A research synthesis of text difficulty and elementary students' reading fluency and comprehension. *Educational Psychology Review, 30*(1), 121–151.

Beltchenko, L. (2020). Talent, ability, and potential: TAPping into the needs of advanced and gifted literacy learners: Intellectual pursuits of young children through picture book literacy, focusing on Italian Preschools. *Illinois Reading Council Journal, 48*(2), 74–86.

Connor, C. M., Piasta, S. B., Fishman, B., Glasney, S., Schatschneider, C., Crowe, E., et al. (2009). Individualizing student instruction precisely: Effects of child by instruction interactions on first graders' literacy development. *Child Development, 80*(1), 77–100. https://doi.org/10.1111/j.1467-8624.2008.01247.x

Mesmer, H. A., Cunningham, J. W., & Hiebert, E. H. (2012). Toward a theoretical model of text complexity for the early grades: Learning from the past, anticipating the future. *Reading Research Quarterly, 47*, 235–258. https://doi.org/10.1002/rrq.019.

MetaMetrics. (2020, April 3). *Understanding Lexile® measures.* https://lexile.com/educators/understanding-lexile-measures.

National Governors Association Center for Best Practices & Council of Chief State School Officers. (2010). *Common core state standards for English language arts and literacy in history/social studies, science, and technical subjects: Appendix A: Research supporting key elements of the standards and glossary of key terms.* Authors.

RAND Reading Study Group. (2002). *Reading for understanding: Toward an R&D program in reading comprehension.* RAND.

Sierschynsk, J., Louie, B., & Pughe, B. (2014). Complexity in picture books. *Reading Teacher*, *68*(4), 287–295.

Valencia, S. W., Wixson, K. K., & Pearson, P. D. (2014). Putting text complexity in context: Refocusing on comprehension of complex text. *The Elementary School Journal*, *115*(2), 270–289. https://doi.org/10.1086/678296.

Wixson, K. K., & Valencia, S. W. (2014). CCSS-ELA suggestions and cautions for addressing text complexity. *Reading Teacher*, *67*(6), 430–434.

Book List

Kalman, M. (2002). *Fireboat: The heroic adventures of the John J. Harvey* (M. Kalman, Illus.). G.P. Putnam's Sons.

Sendak, M. (1984). *Where the wild things are* (M. Sendak, Illus.). Harper & Row.

Zolotow, C. (2007). *The storm book* (M. B. Graham, Illus.). HarperTrophy.

4

Integrating SEL and Subject Content in Lesson Plans

Social and emotional learning is gaining widespread support and implementation throughout K-12 schools, but without a formal place in a school's curriculum and with no presence on standardized and high-stakes assessments, it often must take a back seat to the core subjects and curriculum requirements. However, educators naturally infuse their lessons and interactions with the content and principles of social and emotional learning, from daily greetings and goodbyes to the ways in which they help their students find and share their voice, compassionately listen and disagree, and define their place in their community. Like steps in any familiar process—buckling up a child in a car seat or regularly washing hands—incorporating SEL concepts into their school day is an action that teachers take instinctually.

Taking a step back to recognize how deeply engrained and ever-present SEL components already are will make it easier for teachers to see and make further curricular connections with the core subject content. Picture books that fill the nooks, crannies, and shelves of early elementary classrooms, just as sturdy pots and good cooking implements are found in a well-stocked kitchen, are an ideal tool to help make the intentional connections between subject content and social and emotional domains. Picture books offer myriad examples of characters, feelings, viewpoints, and life experiences to bring to life SEL themes and offer rich content to demonstrate key concepts and starting points for activities.

This chapter will examine how SEL domains and competencies can be integrated throughout the K-3 curricula of social studies, STEM, and English language arts, as well as cross-curricularly in multiple subjects, including the arts. In all three subjects, the SEL themes can be taught both through the subject content and in the exercises and activities of the lessons. The first section of this chapter will give an overview of the SEL domains and competencies of Harvard and CASEL as they relate to the core subjects of social studies, STEM, and English language arts. It will provide examples of how to incorporate SEL themes within the specific subjects using picture books, with differentiation techniques for mixed-ability classrooms. The chapter will conclude with an example of how to build a differentiated lesson that links the SEL themes and the subject content with the use of thoughtfully selected picture books.

Teaching SEL Through Subject Content

Social and emotional themes can be addressed within the curricula of social studies, language arts, and STEM in two ways: through the details of the subject content and through the pedagogy, activities, and exercises of the lessons. The content of the core courses provides a multitude of examples of key social and emotional learning domains and themes for students to examine and discuss. Descriptions of historical, political, and social events are excellent starting places for discussions around the CASEL competencies of responsible decision-making and social awareness. Biographies of leaders, explorers, inventors, artists, and other historically important figures can be tied to such SEL domains as values—how to be a compassionate person who contributes to their community and world in positive ways—and identity—fostering an understanding of the diversity of identities within local and global communities. Details of triumphs of justice and tragedies of injustice provide examples of the CASEL domain of social awareness, which calls for "identifying diverse social norms, including unjust ones . . . recognizing situational demands and opportunities, [and] understanding the influences of organizations and systems on behavior" (CASEL, 2020). Real-life examples of creativity, determination, and persistence provide rich opportunities for SEL lessons around nurturing optimism, courage, gratitude, and hope and developing a growth mindset, grit, and perseverance.

Teaching SEL Through Pedagogy, Activities, and Exercises

In addition to tying SEL lessons to the details of the subject content, social and emotional themes can be powerfully demonstrated through the subjects' pedagogy, activities, and exercises, particularly in hands-on subjects such as STEM classes and art. As students discover, discuss, and demonstrate mastery of the subjects' content details, they can work on projects that help them develop such SEL skills as fostering good communication, working through disagreements and conflicts, and practicing problem-solving. Example activities include peer reviews and class discussions that help students respectfully share their opinions on other students' work and accept others' feedback on their own work, a skill that is included in several of the Common Core standards and is a key part of Harvard's SEL domain of perspective. Class-wide, small group, and individual activities and projects help students develop their executive functioning skills, such as project planning, task initiation, and maintaining attention and focus. Management of conflicts, which are inevitable in any group setting, is a vital SEL skill that children can work on through projects with any size group in all core subjects.

The Role of Picture Books

Picture books are an excellent tool to bridge the subjects' content and pedagogy with SEL domains through the books' plot points, characters' actions and words, and rich illustrations and pictures. A wide variety of fiction and non-fiction genres, including historical fiction, biographies and autobiographies, poetry, graphic novels, and wordless books offer different perspectives and methods of approaching the text. Varying levels of complexity in the text, content matter, and visual presentation provide opportunities for differentiation within the lessons for all levels of students in a mixed-ability classroom. The levels of challenge of the books for students vary through the reading level and amount of text, the use of illustrations and images, and the subject matter. Picture books also offer a natural window into culturally diverse and relevant subject matter.

Table 4.1 gives examples of the Harvard Explore SEL domains and sample questions to use with the picture book

Table 4.1 Harvard Explore SEL Domains and Example Questions

SEL Domain	Sample Questions
Emotion	What emotion was the person/character feeling? Did they use their emotions in a positive or negative way? How would you have felt in that situation?
Cognitive	What steps do you need to take to work on the project [related to the book and lesson]? What materials do you need? What will you do if something does not work the way you expected it to or if you disagree with someone in your group?
Social	How did the people/characters manage a conflict? Was it a good way of managing the conflict? What was the outcome? How did the people/characters communicate with others?
Values	How did the characters show their *values:* what they believed in, what they felt was important, and how they contributed to their community? Were their contributions positive or negative?
Perspectives	What outlooks and beliefs did the person/character have: were they optimistic, courageous, or hopeful? Were they scared and hopeless? Did they show determination, perseverance, or self-confidence?
Identity	How did the people/characters see their place in the world, and how did they demonstrate it through their actions? Did they recognize diversity within their community and throughout the world?

Source: Harvard EASEL Lab. (n.d.) Compare skill focus across frameworks. Harvard Explore SEL. Retrieved from http://exploresel.gse.harvard.edu/compare-domains/

content and corresponding activities. For example, questions that help students think about the SEL domain of emotion focus on having students identify the emotions that the historical figures or characters in the book felt and discuss how the characters acted on those emotions. Students can then consider what emotions they think they would feel in similar circumstances.

Table 4.2 lists the five CASEL competencies and examples of questions related to each. The CASEL competencies are more specifically focused than the Harvard domains and are especially helpful in leading students to think about their own responsibilities and roles in their local and global communities.

The questions related to each domain or competency can be used to tailor the subject content to the SEL themes. The next

Table 4.2 CASEL Domains and Example Questions

SEL Domain	Examples
Self-awareness	How did the emotions and actions of the character/person influence their own behavior? Did they show biases or prejudices? Did they show a growth mindset and sense of purpose?
Self-management	How did the character/people make plans and act on them? Were they courageous in doing things that might have been scary or difficult for them? How did they manage their stress and emotions?
Social Awareness	Did the people/characters show an understanding of other people's perspectives, emotions, and feelings? Did they share their gratitude? Did they realize how other people and organizations have an impact on the world?
Relationship Skills	How did the character/person work with other people? Did they offer support or stand up for other people? Did they have positive relationships with other people? How did they manage conflicts?
Responsible Decision-making	Did the characters/people make good decisions, evaluating the problem and using good judgement to decide how to respond? Did they think about the impact of their decisions on other people and situations?

Source: *CASEL'S SEL Framework: What are the core competence areas and where are they promoted?* (2020). CASEL. Retrieved from www.casel.org/what-is-SEL

section will give examples of how SEL themes can be woven into subject lessons in each of the three core subjects of LA, social studies, and STEM, through both the subject content and the exercises with the use of picture books.

Social Studies

One of the richest subject areas for incorporating SEL themes is social studies. Designed by the National Council for the Social Studies to enhance social studies instruction in K-12 schools, the C3 Framework—College, Career, and Civic Life—for Social Studies State Standards calls for students' education to be driven by helping them learn to "act in ways that promote the common good," a belief that is the foundation of social and emotional learning. Picture books on topics within social studies offer powerful examples of SEL themes that play out through the actions and interactions of people, in historical events, and in the creation and collapse of political, social, and economic institutions. Students can make connections with the characters and events by seeing their own history reflected in the stories, or they can expand their understanding of others' lives and challenges by learning about new life experiences that are very different from their own. Picture books show children as well as adults in roles of heroes and ordinary people, as problem-solvers and advocates, and as flawed, persistent, learning, and growing. Picture books' vivid images in conjunction with the text offer a multitude of opportunities for lesson-building that includes learning opportunities about the events and characters in addition to building critical-thinking skills and integrating SEL concepts such as developing empathy and understanding identity.

A Newbery Medal-winning story that weaves SEL themes into the social studies theme of identity and community is Matt de la Peña's *Last Stop on Market Street*, the story of a grandmother, Nana, and her grandson, CJ, who discuss the differences in the people and settings around them while on a long bus ride. Their conversation and the rich illustrations of the book highlight questions about diversity, inequity, and finding beauty and gratitude during every journey. The book links to numerous SEL competencies and domains and provides powerful questions to examine, including:

- ◆ **Identity:** What did CJ and Nana see on their journey that showed diversity in their community?
- ◆ **Values:** How might CJ's experiences help him to become a compassionate person who contributes to his community?
- ◆ **Perspectives:** What did CJ's assumptions about the other people on his trip say about biases, prejudices, or other beliefs that he might hold?
- ◆ **Social awareness:** Did CJ show empathy and compassion for the people he saw on his journey? How did that change when they reached their destination?

A non-fiction social studies topic that is powerfully presented in picture books is social advocacy, especially the Civil Rights Movement. *Let The Children March* by Monica Clark-Robinson, which won the American Library Association's Coretta Scott King Illustrator Honor, and *The Youngest Marcher: The Story of Audrey Faye Hendricks, A Young Civil Rights Activist* by Cynthia Levinson tell the story of the 1963 Children's March in Birmingham, Alabama, in which children marched to demand desegregation, resulting in the arrest of more than 3,000 young people. The books offer inspirational stories of children showing enormous courage and initiative in the face of violence and their own imprisonment. The two books link to numerous SEL competencies and domains and provide powerful questions to examine, including:

- ◆ **Emotions:** What emotions were the children feeling before, during, and after their involvement in the marches?
- ◆ **Values:** How did the children make positive changes in the world? Why did they decide to take action?
- ◆ **Identity:** How did the children's actions illustrate their sense of identity? How do these stories show diversity within our world?

- **Social awareness:** What aspects of social awareness, such as showing leadership, offering support, and standing up for the rights of others, were demonstrated in these stories?

The themes and images of these books can be intimidating and possibly frightening to children because of the books' straightforward illustration of how the children were mistreated by adults, and younger children may struggle to understand that experience and how they can relate to it. Bringing the idea of civic participation down to the level of the classroom, school, and community can help students understand how such heroic and historical experiences can link to their own lives. Exercises for the lesson can involve talking to students about what they think needs to be changed within their own lives and why, then making a plan for how they can convince people to make the change. Students could lead a recycling drive at their school or talk about hunger and food scarcity—how to ensure that everyone gets food while none gets wasted in the lunch room. The lesson that change can begin with every individual, with small steps and good intentions, will support many SEL domains.

STEM

Of the three core subjects discussed in this book, STEM content may appear at first to be the most challenging to link to SEL themes. The Next Generation Science Standards include such topics as forces and interactions (kindergarten), structure and properties of matter (second grade), independent relationships in ecosystems (second grade), engineering design (grades K-2), and heredity (third grade). At first glance it could be difficult to imagine integrating SEL themes such as ethical values or hope and gratitude with teaching these scientific topics. But the rich themes of picture books provide a creative way to link together the STEM topic content with SEL competencies. Biographies of groundbreaking scientists, engineers, technologists, and mathematicians provide a wide variety of opportunities to look at SEL themes such as fostering perseverance, grit, and creativity; developing cognitive skills such as goal-setting; good decision-making; working through challenges and learning from failure; defining one's identity; and building skills around self and social awareness. The stories of important STEM events, discoveries, and inventions offer opportunities to link in SEL themes that are relevant to the events; for example, ingenuity, creativity, teamwork, conflict management, and time management were crucial in overcoming some of the crises during early space exploration. A wide variety of books that show everyday people and kids using creativity, ingenuity, and perseverance to achieve their goals or complete a task are a great source of inspiration within the sciences.

Linda, a K-3 science teacher and leader of her school's GEMS (Girls in Engineering, Math, and Science) club, described how she linked the content from the Next Generation Science Standards' Biological Evolution: Unity and Diversity topic to a main theme for SEL for that week: "In my second grade science class we just connected our Living Things Unit and learning about the sizes of hearts and animals with one heart, three hearts, and no hearts to how a kind heart helps us as well for our Random Acts of Kindness Week."

Creative connections such as Linda's link between the SEL theme of kindness and her science lesson offer a wonderful opportunity to bring SEL themes into the STEM classroom. For example, *The Lion's Share: A Tale of Halving Cake and Eating It, Too* by Matthew McElligott offers math explanations along with lessons in kindness and sharing through the story of an ant invited to have dinner with a lion king. The other guests, which include a beetle, frog, warthog, and hippo, are poorly behaved, and when the cake is brought out, the animals each take half of it for themselves, dividing it into smaller and smaller sections until none is left for the king. Once they realize their greedy mistakes, the animal guests promise to bring treats for the king the next day, each trying to outdo the others by promising double the number of treats of the previous animal, ending with the elephant. "The elephant was crestfallen, but he had to top the hippo. Elephants were twice as good as hippos. With a deep breath, he announced,

'And I, the great elephant, shall bake twice as many as the hippo. Two hundred and forty-six peanut butter pound cakes!'" The book ties together the math concepts with lessons on sharing, kindness, and generosity. The SEL themes that run through *The Lion's Share* include:

- ◆ **Self-awareness:** Was the animals' behavior kind or selfish? How did they treat each other?
- ◆ **Relationship skills:** Were the animals showing good examples of teamwork and sharing? Were they acting positively towards each other?
- ◆ **Responsible decision-making:** Did the animals make good decisions? Which animal(s) made better decisions? What were the consequences of the animals' decisions?

Cognitive SEL skills in STEM. A strong link between SEL themes and STEM content can also be found in the exercises and activities of the subjects. Completion of STEM activities requires cognitive skills, such as goal setting, task initiation, and time management as well as problem-solving and learning from failure. Group activities require the development and use of good communication skills among the students: dividing up roles and responsibilities; assigning tasks; meeting goals and deadlines; and providing support, encouragement, and understanding throughout the project, but especially during challenging periods. To supplement the activities, hands-on and how-to stories offer inspiring and humorous lessons to show how to approach and overcome challenges and accept failures.

A number of popular books that show examples of ingenuity and creativity provide wonderful opportunities for prompting creative brainstorming and inspiring hands-on activities, whether in a structured lesson or a more open maker-space setting. *If I Built A Car* and *If I Built A House* by Chris Van Dusen and the Questioneers book series by Andrea Beaty, which includes *Rosie Revere, Engineer*; *Ada Twist, Scientist*; and *Iggy Peck, Architect*, inspire creativity and brainstorming, as well as SEL skills such as problem-solving, creative planning, and construction, prompting questions of "What if . . . ?," "How can I . . . ?," and "How does this work?"

Douglas, You're A Genius! by Ged Adamson tells the story of a girl, Nancy, and her dog, Douglas, who accidentally send their ball through a hole in their fence into the next yard and receive it back with a note in an unfamiliar language (Spanish), setting off an adventure to reach the other side and meet the note's sender. Through problem-solving and trial and error, the pair come up with a solution to get to the other side of the fence and joyfully meet their neighbors. *Rosie Revere, Engineer* uses rhymes to tell the story of a girl who was laughed at for her creative inventions but who finds encouragement and inspiration from an aunt:

> "'Your brilliant first flop was a raging success!
> Come on, let's get busy and on to the next!'
> She handed a notebook to Rosie Revere,
> who smiled at her aunt as it all became clear.
> Life might have its failures, but this was *not* it.
> The only true failure can come if you quit."

The SEL themes that run through these stories include:

- **Cognitive:** How did Douglas and Nancy try to get over/under/through this fence? (These questions can tie in the scientific theories and discussion.) What materials did they need? What are some examples of their problem-solving? How did Rosie respond to failure?
- **Perspective:** What perspectives did Douglas and Nancy show while trying to get to the other side of the fence? Did they show perseverance?
- **Self-management:** How did Nancy, Douglas, and Rosie set goals for themselves? How did they manage their own emotions? How did Rosie take initiative in deciding on her inventions?
- **Responsible decision-making:** How did Nancy, Douglas, and Rosie demonstrate good decision-making skills, like curiosity and open-mindedness? Did they consider the best way to achieve their goals before making decisions on how to proceed?

English Language Arts

With a breadth of content of course material, there are innumerable opportunities to teach social and emotional learning within language arts, and the integration of picture books into the lessons is a natural step. CASEL published a guide to integrating each of their five core SEL competencies with elementary ELA instruction (CASEL, 2017), providing examples both of teaching SEL skills through the specific content and as general competencies in the exercises. For example, they suggest using ELA time to help foster self-awareness and self-management skills such as self-calming, focusing, and time management. Within the ELA content, CASEL suggests focusing on the SEL competency of social awareness by having students take the perspective of characters within stories and practicing empathy for their challenges, life experiences, and outlooks (CASEL, 2017).

A beautiful book on the theme of empathy and kindness is *Adrian Simcox Does NOT Have a Horse* by Marcy Campbell, which tells the story of a daydreaming boy, Adrian, who describes his beautiful horse to a doubtful and unkind classmate, Chloe. When she visits Adrian's house and understands the reasons behind his imaginary creation she learns a lesson in compassion and empathy. Though the story is told in the first person through Chloe's point of view, Adrian's feelings and motivations are made clear, and the beautiful illustrations give voice to the boy's imagination. This book is an excellent starting point for the sample lesson from CASEL (2020) that suggests activities such as identifying the characters' feelings, having the students discuss in small groups the influence of emotions on our actions, and talking about how characters' feelings and points of view affect others and the story's resolution. The SEL themes that run through the story include:

- ◆ **Emotion:** What emotions does Chloe have, and how does she express them? What are Adrian's emotions? How do the characters' emotions change throughout the book, and why?

- **Social:** How does Chloe communicate with Adrian? How does she play with and interact with him? What words would you use to describe the way that Chloe treats Adrian in the beginning, middle, and end of the book?
- **Self-awareness:** Does Chloe show any biases or prejudices in the way she talks about Adrian? Do those change by the end of the book?

Wordless Picture Books

Using wordless books in ELA lessons creates opportunities for children to develop comprehension, vocabulary, and expression skills to understand and discuss the story in their own words. By placing the focus solely on the images in the book, children can see the importance of the images, with each child drawing on different views and aspects of the pictures to retell the story in their own words.

I Walk With Vanessa: A Story About a Simple Act of Kindness is a wordless book by a French illustrator-author team writing under the pen-name Kerascoët. It tells the story, through beautifully drawn pictures, of a girl who is bullied on the way to school. Her neighbor sees the incident from afar and befriends her the next day, gathering friends from the neighborhood to walk with them to school. *Wolf in the Snow* by Matthew Cordell, which won the 2018 Caldecott Award, is the story of girl on her way home from school who helps a lost wolf cub find his way back to his family. When she finds herself lost in the snowstorm as she tries to make her way back home, the wolves return her kindness and help her family find her. Both *I Walk With Vanessa* and *Wolf in the Snow* vividly portray their characters' emotions, values, and kindness through their illustrations alone, highlighting the anger on Vanessa's bully's face and the fear on the faces of the wolf cub and the girl. Students can identify and label the emotions that the characters feel and discuss such SEL themes as gratitude, compassion, kindness, and empathy.

Cross-Curricular Lessons

The themes and topics of social studies and science often overlap and dovetail, allowing for opportunities to teach both subjects through a single lesson or across multiple periods of the day. Science and social studies may not have a prominent place within the curriculum of early elementary classrooms, so cross-curricular connections help educators address that content more efficiently.

Social Studies and Science Links

Biographies of environmentalists and conservationists in STEM provide a natural link with the topic of advocacy movements in social studies. One example is *The Tree Lady: The True Story of How One Tree-Loving Woman Changed a City Forever* by H. Joseph Hopkins, which tells the true story of Kate Sessions, who led the transformation of the heart of San Diego from a treeless desert to the lush parkland of Balboa Park in time for San Diego's 1915 Panama-California Exposition. The story describes and provides vibrant illustrations of the horticultural details of the process, including how Kate selected and gathered seedlings that would flourish, along with her organization of an environmental advocacy movement to plant thousands of trees and plants. In addition to the scientific details of how Sessions and her trees transformed the environment, the story also details Sessions' personal life, which is filled with SEL teaching opportunities around the topics of citizenship, values, ethics, perspective, and perseverance. *The Tree Lady* will be discussed in more detail in Chapter 6, Integrating SEL and Social Studies, which includes a sample lesson plan that uses the book.

Social Studies and Language Arts

Two biography picture books offer inspiring stories of two remarkable women centered around the topic of reading and literacy that fit perfectly into LA while also supporting social studies topics. *The Oldest Student: How Mary Walker Learned to Read* by Rita L. Hubbard tells the story of Mary Walker, who was born into slavery in Alabama and freed at the age of 15 but worked to support her family her entire life and never had a chance to go to school. At the age of 114 she had outlived her entire family and found herself alone and yearning to read for herself. "For the next year and a half, Mary put everything she had into learning to read. It wasn't easy; after all, she was the oldest student in the class—and probably in the entire country." Through remarkable determination, Mary learned to read and was celebrated by her community, by US presidents, and with a historical marker at her home, where she died at the age of 121.

Planting Stories: The Life of Librarian and Storyteller Pura Belpré by Anika Aldamuy Denise tells the story of Pura Belpré, a Puerto Rican author and storyteller who came to New York and began working in the New York Public Library. When she found that there were no Spanish-language books or stories, she wrote them herself, created a collection of Spanish-language books for the New York Public Library, and shared them with the Spanish-language community. "Now a published author, puppeteer and storyteller, Pura travels from branch to branch, classroom to classroom, to churches and community centers . . . planting her story seeds in the hearts and minds of children new to this island who wish to remember *la lengua y los colores* of home." Upon her death in 1982, the American Library Association created an annual award in Pura's name that honors outstanding works of literature by Latinx authors and illustrators.

Mary's and Pura's stories offer a wealth of lessons in both social studies and language arts, tied in with powerful SEL lessons. The themes of the power of literacy and the value of maintaining one's first language can support a number of ELA Common Core standards at the same time they are conveying these powerful messages. The details of Mary's life as a freed slave facing enormous hardships provide a powerful social studies lesson. Pura's story of immigrating to the United States and singlehandedly creating and sharing a collection of Spanish-language stories and capturing traditional folktales of her native Puerto Rico offers a number of lessons around immigration and the diversity of the United States. With Spanish text and phrases used throughout the text, the book also serves as a bridge for Spanish-speaking children.

The SEL themes that run through the stories include:

- ◆ **Perspectives:** How did Pura and Mary demonstrate courage, grit, and resilience?

- **Self-management:** How did Pura and Mary set personal goals and show courage to meet those goals?
- **Self-awareness:** How did Pura and Mary develop their interests and show a sense of purpose?

Social Studies and Art

Picture books with a focus on art also provide opportunities for a cross-curricular link with social studies or art. One example is *Stepping Stones: A Refugee Family's Journey*, written by Margriet Ruurs and illustrated by a Syrian artist, Nizar Ali Badr; it is a bilingual (English/Arabic) book that tells the story of a family forced to leave their war-torn country as refugees. The book uses illustrations of Ali Badr's stone-based art pieces to creatively represent the life, hardships, and journey that a family endures to find a safe home in another country. The book includes a list of organizations that help refugees, and a portion of the proceeds from the book are donated to resettlement organizations in North America. The power of the book lies not only in the moving story and Ali Badr's own story but in the integration of the art as a component of the story and a unique method of illustrating the text.

Illustrations are a powerful piece of the story in *Drawn Together*, written by Minh Lê and illustrated by the Caldecott Medal-winning illustrator and author Dan Santat. It tells the story in a paneled format with rich illustrations and minimal words of a young boy who struggles to connect with his Vietnamese grandfather who looks after him. After struggling with differences in language, food preferences, and entertainment, the boy and his grandfather notice that they share a love of art. "Right when I gave up on talking, my grandfather surprised me by revealing a world beyond words," the boy says. The two draw glorious scenes of battling warriors and fierce dragons, finding a connection in their art. "Now, after years of searching for the right words, we find ourselves happily. . . . SPEECHLESS."

The two books share SEL themes of identity and community, empathy, emotions, and social SEL domains such as communicating and interacting with others. Questions that teachers can share with students related to SEL themes in these books include:

- What struggles did the boy and his grandfather in *Drawn Together* have in communicating, and how did they overcome those challenges?
- What emotions do you think the refugees in *Stepping Stones* were feeling?
- What challenges and worries do you think the refugees will have when they arrive in their new homes? What would you say to them if you met them?

Differentiation

There are multiple ways to differentiate the lessons for students with a range of abilities and interests in mixed-ability classrooms. One method is adding breadth to the content coverage by integrating additional books or materials with different viewpoints on the same general topic. For example, tying into the theme of young activists, *Brave Girl: Clara and the Shirtwaist Makers' Strike of 1909* by Michele Markel tells the story of Clara Lemlich, who went to work in a garment factory and led walkouts to protest the working conditions, resulting in her repeated arrests. She eventually led the largest walkout of women workers in US history and succeed in gaining better working conditions. The book complements *The Youngest Marcher* and *Let the Children March* by showing another advocacy movement led by a marginalized group, in this case, young women workers. Additional reference books can be provided to provide more context and details of other advocacy movements.

Bringing in books at higher and lower reading levels is a second method of providing differentiation in the lesson. A book at a higher reading level that could be brought into the lesson with Kate Sessions is *Wangari Maathai: The Woman Who Planted Millions of Trees* by Franck Prévot, which tells the story of Kenyan political activist and environmentalist Wangari Maathai, who was the first African woman to receive the Nobel Peace Prize. She founded the Green Belt Movement to stop the deforestation of Africa and, like Kate Sessions, led a tree-planting initiative that resulted in a transformation of the native landscape with more than 30 million trees planted. Wangari later joined a movement to establish a democratic government in Kenya, providing a powerful link to a social studies lesson. For a lower reading level, *Wangari's Trees of Peace* by Jeanette Winter or *Mama Miti: Wangari Maathai and the Trees of Kenya* by Donna Jo Napoli provide more versions of Wangari Maathai's life. The stories of the two remarkable women's efforts and success, and the social and emotional skills that they used to achieve their accomplishments, provide a way to compare and contrast their experiences and responses. *We Planted a Tree* by Diane Muldrow, *The Tiny Seed* by Eric Carle, *In the Garden* by Emma Giuliani, and *Who Will Plant a Tree?* by Jerry Pallotta are a few of the many examples of books that offer a broader look at the same topic.

Designing a Lesson Plan

The starting point of building a lesson can be either the core subject content or the SEL theme, and from there the content and SEL theme can be linked through the selection of a picture book. For example, starting with a social studies unit on a historical figure or event, teachers can pull out SEL themes such as empathy, perspective, and identity, then create questions or activities around those SEL domains through a picture book on the topic. Starting with an SEL theme such as emotions or cognitive skills, teachers can build out a unit within one of the core subjects, such as science or ELA, supported by a picture book. Later chapters in this book will give specific examples of building lessons with correlations to curricular standards in social studies, STEM, and ELA, with lists of leveled picture books divided by content topics and SEL themes and sample lesson plans. This section will provide a template of how to create a general differentiated lesson using picture books and SEL themes.

There are generally four stages of the lesson, and the duration of each stage can be adjusted based on the time available and the complexity of the topic. The first stage is typically a group activity that is focused on the SEL topic, followed by a whole-group read of a book on the content topic and SEL theme. However, in many cases the lesson works well with switching the order of those stages, putting the book reading first, followed by the group activity. In the third stage in the lesson, students will complete activities that are differentiated to allow students flexibility in selecting a project that is well-suited to their interests and abilities. The final stage in the lesson is bringing the whole group back together to reflect on the SEL theme and content topic.

Stage 1: Group Activity (1 Day)

This activity, which typically takes a single class period, is an introduction of the SEL theme that highlights the students' knowledge of and feelings about the theme. For example, a lesson that focuses on empathy could present a real or imagined disagreement from the playground or lunchroom and ask students to consider how other students feel and the assumptions that we make about others; a lesson about responsible decision-making could begin by asking students to build a tower with limited materials. This group activity requires the students to work cooperatively, drawing on executive functioning skills, good communication, management of emotions, and task planning and completion. This group activity is typically followed by a group reflection in which students share their experiences during the activity with the class, in a discussion format or by responding to a writing prompt.

Stage 2: Whole-Group Read of a Relevant Text With Activities (2–3 Days)

The next stage is the whole group reading of a text related to the content and SEL theme. This stage in the process serves to unite the class around a common "anchor text." In the next stage, when the students participate in the differentiated learning activities as individuals or in small groups, this text "anchors" the large group of students to common ideas. This whole group read is also the ideal time for some version of direct instruction, where the educator makes sure the students are understanding key information or developing necessary skills.

There are numerous ways to approach a whole group read-aloud. Educators may decide to "think aloud" as they read, pausing occasionally to describe what they are thinking about. This process allows the educators to model what good readers do as they read and also to guide the students' thinking in the direction of the intended lesson goals. An educator might also outline a series of discussion questions and allow the students to discuss with their "elbow partners" on the rug or the children sitting with them in their table groups. Children can then be asked to share their thinking with the whole class.

Another powerful teaching option is a dialogic reading of the core text. The teacher reads the book with the class, pausing to ask questions and to support the students' knowledge of key vocabulary in the story. The CROWD strategy for developing increasingly complex questions is helpful, which moves from simple completion questions to the distancing questions that look at more complex connections: text-to-self, which has the students link the story to their own experiences; text-to-text, which has them compare stories—a requirement of the Common Core ELA standards; text-to-world, which draws on more complicated understandings of how the text's plot or characters/people relate to what the students already know; and text-to-graphics, which links the text's illustrations and images to how the students are visualizing the text (Hynes-Berry, 2012). The five stages of this strategy are:

- ◆ **Completion questions:** "Little Red Riding Hood was going to visit her _____."
- ◆ **Recall questions:** "What happened when Little Red Riding Hood first met the wolf?"
- ◆ **Open-ended questions:** "What message do you think the author wanted us to learn from the text?"
- ◆ **W questions:** "Who? What? Where? When? Why?"
- ◆ **Distancing questions** that relate the text-to-self, text-to-text, text-to-world, such as: "Was there ever a time you didn't listen to your mom or dad and it caused you trouble? Does this book remind you of any others we've read? How is this book similar to/different from things that happen in the real world?"

The CROWD questions can be adjusted to meet the content and SEL themes of the lesson. The SEL questions found earlier in this chapter are a good starting point.

This second stage of the lesson is flexible and can be completed in two class periods or spread across as much as a week (assuming one class period per day) if there are longer pieces, group activities, or if the students are allowed to choose multiple activities. Optional extensions include a small group read of the text where students write their responses on self-adhesive notes. A bibliotherapy approach would include a discussion of the challenges and emotions that the characters face. Identifying and naming the emotions helps with a universalization that shows children that these challenges are shared by many.

The activities that follow the group reading pull in the relevant SEL theme. For example, focusing on the SEL skill of empathy, the CASEL competency of social awareness calls on students to "understand the perspectives of and empathize with others, including those from diverse backgrounds, cultures, and contexts" (CASEL, n.d.). This includes showing compassion, empathy, gratitude, and concern for others and recognizing other people's strengths and perspectives. More broadly, the competency calls for looking at the influences of diverse social norms, situational demands, and organizations and systems on behaviors and outcomes, including injustices. This competency is supported by a wide variety of activities within a lesson plan, such as:

- After reading a biography of a historically important figure (tied to a social studies or STEM topic), identify their beliefs, motivations, and emotions. How did they react in a given situation or to a challenge—what emotions were they feeling? How do the students think they would have felt if they were in that situation?
- After reading a story about an important historical event, describe the situation that led up to the event. For example, why did an event such as a political rebellion or the Civil Rights Movement take place? What led to a discovery or invention? How did the people involved in the

event feel leading up to it, and why did that lead to the occurrence of the event?
- ◆ After sharing a story about a movement for change, discuss the factors that led people to get involved. What were their feelings, and how did they act on them? What was the outcome? Then have the students come up with a problem within their own school or community and think about the causes of the problem and brainstorm solutions for change.
- ◆ Retelling and reenacting the stories through standard acting, reader's theater, and narrative pantomime, in which students act out the text silently as the teacher reads it aloud, are powerful ways for students to process and show their understanding of stories.

Stage 3: Differentiated Learning (2–3 Days)

The third stage of the lesson includes differentiated activities in which students can apply their learning at different ability and interest levels. Areas for differentiation include the use of different texts (by topic or difficulty, as described earlier), reading individually or in small groups, offering differing types of teacher support, and using audio books. A choice board in which students pick one activity from each column allows the teacher to ensure that a student works on an activity that addresses each of the key learning goals while also offering students choice about the content and type of activity. Table 4.3 shows a sample choice board.

Hynes-Berry (2012) describes a classroom activity she led that involved an initial whole-group reading of the book followed by her splitting the students into four groups. The first group had a narrator read the opening part of the text while the rest of the group pantomimed the actions; the second group drew a picture of the next section of the story, either as a single mural or in separate panels; the third group acted out a section of the story with music and movement; and the fourth group made simple puppets and acted out the final scene. Her division of the class into small groups also allowed for differentiation based on the students' interests and abilities.

Table 4.3 Example of a Choice Board for a Lesson

Choice Board: Choose one from each column.

Choose 1	Choose 1	Choose 1
Draw 2 pictures—the main problem and the solution. Add labels if you can.	Choose 4 words you did not know from your book. Write the words, and draw a picture for each that shows what it means.	Make a list of 5 emotion words from the story, and draw a face that shows each emotion.
Draw a picture of the main character solving the problem. Write what the problem was and how the character solved it.	Choose 4 words you did know from your book. Write a sentence for each that shows you know what it means.	Describe or draw the emotions of one of the main characters in the story. How did their feelings change throughout the story?
Write a paragraph in which you describe what you know about the main character and how his/her traits impacted the main events in the story.	Write an acrostic poem for a word from your book. The word will be the idea that runs vertically. The words that come from the letters will show the meaning.	Draw a cartoon with at least 5 panels that tells a story in which one character shows empathy for another.

Stage 4: Revisit Group Activity (1 Day)

In the final stage of the lesson, the group revisits the initial group activity with a closure or reflection. Teachers put the students into small, mixed-ability groups and have them reflect on what they've learned, starting the students off with prompts and two or three key questions that structure the conversation. Using the example of empathy, questions could include: How did the characters in your books show empathy? What can you learn from these characters about how to show empathy? Once the students have completed their tasks in small groups, the teacher pulls them back together, and each group shares what they discussed. This stage concludes with a full-group reflection on the subject content, the SEL theme, and the picture book, tying into the students' thoughts and experiences on how those themes fit into their own world.

This lesson template is broad and flexible and can be adjusted based on the availability of time, resources, and materials, as well as the ability levels and interests of the students. Thoughtful selection of the picture books provides culturally relevant content, including bilingual and multilingual materials. The next chapters will provide specific examples of creating lessons for social studies, science, and ELA with links to SEL through picture books. Each subject-related chapter will give content details, examples of texts, and a lesson plan and book list.

References

CASEL: History. (n.d.). CASEL. Retrieved from https://casel.org/history/

CASEL'S SEL Framework: What are the core competence areas and where are they promoted? (2020). CASEL. Retrieved from www.casel.org/what-is-SEL

Harvard EASEL Lab. (n.d.). Compare skill focus across frameworks. *Harvard Explore SEL*. http://exploresel.gse.harvard.edu/compare-domains/

Hynes-Berry, M., & Chen, J.-Q. (2012). *Don't leave the story in the book: Using literature to guide inquiry in early childhood classrooms.* Teachers College Press.

Book List

Beaty, A. (2013). *Rosie Revere, engineer* (D. Roberts, Illus.). Abrams Books for Young Readers.

Beaty, A. (2016a). *Iggy Peck, architect* (D. Roberts, Illus.). Abrams Books for Young Readers.

Beaty, A. (2016b). *Ada Twist, scientist* (D. Roberts, Illus.). Abrams Books for Young Readers.

Campbell, M. (2018). *Adrian Simcox does not have a horse* (C. Luyken, Illus.). Dial Books.

Carle, E. (1970). *The tiny seed*. Little Simon.

Clark-Robinson, M. (2018). *Let the children march* (F. Morrison, Illus.). Clarion Books.

Cordell, M. (2017). *Wolf in the snow*. Feiwel & Friends.

Denise, A. A. (2020a). *Planting stories: The life of librarian and storyteller Pura Belpré* (P. Escobar, Illus.). HarperCollins.

Denise, A. A. (2020b). *Sembrando historias: Pura Belpré: bibliotecaria y narradora de cuentos: Planting stories: The life of librarian and storyteller Pura Belpré* (P. Escobar, Illus.). HarperCollins Espanol.

Dusen, C. V. (2007). *If I built a car*. Puffin Books.

Dusen, C. V. (2019). *If I built a house*. Puffin Books.

Giuliani, E. (2020). *In the garden*. Princeton Architectural Press.

Hopkins, H. J. (2013). *The tree lady: The true story of how one tree-loving woman changed a city forever* (J. McElmurry, Illus.). Simon & Schuster.

Hubbard, R. L. (2020). *The oldest student: How Mary Walker learned to read* (O. Mora, Illus.). Anne Schwartz Books.

Kerascoët. (2018). *I walk with Vanessa: A picture book story about a simple act of kindness*. Schwartz & Wade.

Lê, M. (2018). *Drawn together* (D. Santat, Illus.). Little, Brown Books for Young Readers.

Levinson, C. (2017). *The youngest marcher: The story of Audrey Faye Hendricks, a young civil rights activist* (V. Brantley-Newton, Illus.). Atheneum Books for Young Readers.

Muldrow, D. (2016). *We planted a tree* (B. Staake, Illus.). Dragonfly Books.

Napoli, D. J. (2010). *Mama Miti: Wangari Maathai and the trees of Kenya* (K. Nelson, Illus.). Simon & Schuster/Paula Wiseman Books.

Pallotta, J. (2010). *Who will plant a tree?* (T. Leonard, Illus.). Sleeping Bear Press.

Peña, M. de la. (2015). *Last stop on Market Street* (C. Robinson, Illus.). G.P. Putnam's Sons Books for Young Readers.

Rosenstock, B. (2014). *The noisy paint box: The colors and sounds of Kandinsky's abstract art* (M. GrandPre, Illus.). Knopf Books for Young Readers.

Ruurs, M., & Badr, N. A. (2016). *Stepping stones: A refugee family's journey* (F. Raheem, Trans.; N.A. Badr, Illus.). Orca Book Publishers.

Winter, J. (2018). *Wangari's trees of peace: A true story from Africa*. Clarion Books.

5

Integrating SEL and STEM Using Picture Books

In *Pattan's Pumpkin*, a story from the Irular tribe in Southern India, a farmer named Pattan finds a wilting plant in the valley and lovingly tends to it. To his amazement, a vast pumpkin grows from the vine, sprouting larger and larger, taller than the goats, fatter than the pigs, higher than the elephants, and reaching towards the mountains themselves. When a fierce rainstorm brews overhead and threatens to flood the valley, Pattan wonders whether the massive pumpkin can serve as a shelter for all of the life in his land—the seeds and saplings, his farm animals and the area's wildlife, and Pattan and his wife, Kanni. As the storm rages, Pattan and the animals hollow out the pumpkin and climb inside, and Kanni joins him with samples of their grains, seeds, and herbs. They wait out the storm inside the pumpkin, eventually returning safely with their animals and plants to their home in the valley in the foothills of the Sahyadri Mountains, where their descendants live today (Soundar, 2017).

The story of Pattan's pumpkin is one of many variations of the *flood myth*, a story that describes a flood that destroys entire civilizations, typically as divine retribution. The earliest versions of the flood myth date back to ancient Babylonia, around 2000–1600 BC, and the story is found in the religious texts of Christianity, Judaism, Hinduism, and Islam, as well as in the historical writings of the ancient Greeks, indigenous peoples of North and South America, Africa, and Australia, and in Mesopotamian, Irish, Norse, and Polynesian myths and legends (Chen, 2013; Dundes, 1988). Though the story is clearly a fantastical tale, numerous historical flooding events in areas from Mesopotamia to the Mediterranean, India, and the Americas likely informed and supported the spread and popularity of the flood myth throughout historical and literary traditions (Frazer, 2013).

Myths, legends, and *pourquoi* stories, which explain how things came to be, are archetypes of stories that reoccur in multiple cultures throughout history. These stories contain themes, plots, and characters that are deeply rooted in our shared discourse and understandings of the world. Many stories offer explanations for natural disasters or natural occurrences such as the changing of the seasons, the habits and appearance of animals, and the rising and setting of the sun and moon. They are rich in description and can be reassuring in their explanations, uplifting in their solutions, and frightening in their visions of destructive forces and malevolent beings.

These stories are the foundation of picture books that are a starting point for discussions and learning opportunities, in this case around scientific and natural forces and occurrences. Core mathematical and scientific concepts lie at the heart of many beloved children's stories, from Goldilocks' comparisons of temperature, size, and comfort to the relative strengths of the Three Little Pigs' construction materials. Attributes, comparisons, measurements, patterns, and other mathematical and scientific concepts are key components of the stories. Children can compare sizes, shapes, lengths, and other empirical measurements through the words and experiences of their beloved characters. Fantastical situations, such as Jack's beanstalk, Rapunzel's hair, and a princess's sensitivity to an uncomfortable bed, are fictional and unscientific in their details but serve as engaging and imaginative discussion and lesson starters.

Using these picture books to bring together scientific content and social and emotional themes is a natural step and powerful tool in elementary classrooms. The characters and plotlines of children's stories offer myriad opportunities to explore SEL themes, such as supporting problem-solving and decision-making; developing good communication and conflict management; fostering ethical values, courage, gratitude, optimism, and perseverance; and nurturing a compassionate and ethical self-identity and sense of responsibility in the world.

The details of the flood myth vary between versions, but every account maintains three key elements: the diversity of life, nature's power and potential for destruction, and the heroic efforts to plan and carry out a massive rescue and survival of the catastrophe. Themes of life sciences, weather and natural forces, and social, cognitive, and emotional competencies are interwoven through the story, including such topics and questions as:

- **Living things and their environment:** What plants and animals live in the area? What do they look like, what do they eat, and what is their habitat? What do they need for the journey? How would they interact?
- **Weather:** What are the forces of nature, and how do they have an impact on the environment and living things within it? What types of weather patterns are nearby, and how do they affect us?
- **Measurements and scientific hypotheses:** How much space do the animals need? How much would they weigh? How much room would their food take up?
- **Cognitive skills, decision-making, problem-solving, and executive functioning skills:** What are the steps you would need to take and questions you should ask to plan a rescue of so many living things?

Embedding core SEL concepts within subject lessons, such as in the example of *Pattan's Pumpkin*, is especially important within the fields of STEM—science, technology, engineering, and math—to ensure that all students have equal opportunities and self-confidence to find success in those subjects. More than any other core academic subject, the path to success in STEM courses is fraught with obstacles and inequalities that begin to develop in early elementary school settings. Girls' interest in STEM subjects begins to drop at the age of 10, with 12.7% of girls indicating an interest in pursuing STEM-related careers at the point of high school graduation, compared to 39.7% of boys (Wieselmann, Roehrig, & Kim, 2020). Women are less likely than men to opt for STEM educational programs, to hold a degree in STEM subjects, and to enter the labor force in the field of STEM. Once in a STEM profession, women face pay inequity, gender stereotypes regarding their abilities and commitment to their jobs, and other obstacles to their success, which, in turn, negatively affect their work engagement and career confidence (van Veelen et al., 2019). Advancements have been made towards an equitable representation of women in STEM jobs, with 50% of all STEM jobs (including health-related jobs) held by women overall, but a substantial inequity remains in jobs in physical sciences (where only 40% are held by women), computing (25% held by women), and engineering (15% held by women). Only 9% of STEM jobs are held by Black workers, and 8% by Latinx workers (Zewe, 2021).

Internal barriers such as anxiety, low self-esteem, and low academic confidence are both the cause and the result of the external, systemic inequalities in STEM enrollment and success. Math anxiety, which can begin in the earliest elementary grades, inhibits students' math achievement in informal class settings, formative and high-stakes assessments, and in everyday mathematical tasks, resulting in low math achievement and avoidance of math-related courses, tasks, and careers (Gunderson et al., 2018; Ramirez, Shaw, & Maloney, 2018). The fear of failure can itself lead to failure, which then perpetuates a cycle of anxiety, avoidance, and poor performance.

The importance of teaching social and emotional learning in conjunction with STEM content starting in the early elementary grades is a crucial step in expanding access to STEM courses and fostering participation and success in STEM-focused classes and careers. Solutions include reinforcing foundational SEL beliefs such as self-confidence, acceptance of failure, grit, and resilience, and fostering values that encourage acceptance of all students into the courses, through such SEL competencies as taking others' perspectives, recognizing strengths in others, practicing teamwork, and offering support and standing up for the rights of others.

SEL themes can be taught in STEM courses by highlighting SEL themes in the content and by supporting the development of SEL competencies through the activities and interactions of the students in STEM courses. Stories serve as the connection that links SEL and STEM curriculum—through both existing stories and stories that students create as part of the lessons. Having students create and solve story problems in STEM offers an additional opportunity to present key concepts in contextualized, real-world examples to complement generic, abstract representations of the math concepts (Kaminski, Sloutsky, & Heckler, 2008; Kaminski & Sloutsky, 2020).

This chapter will address three main areas of STEM: science, mathematics, and technology, using the standards for each subject: the Next Generation Science Standards, the Common Core Standards for Mathematics, and the technology standards from the International Society for Technology in Education (ISTE). Each section of the chapter will highlight the correlations between the standards and SEL domains and competencies and will provide examples of specific stories and associated lesson plans for different aspects of the core subjects.

Science

The Next Generation Science Standards call on students to ask questions; develop and use models; plan and carry out investigations; analyze and interpret data; engage in argument using evidence; and obtain, evaluate, and communicate information (NGSS Lead States, 2013). While these capabilities and aptitudes largely rely on skills within the cognitive domain of social and emotional learning, they also require students to develop skill sets that fall into SEL competencies such as self-awareness, self-management, and responsible decision-making. Table 5.1 provides examples of correlations between the Next Generation Science Standards and SEL domains that run through the standards and can be incorporated in the lessons and exercises.

Table 5.1 Sample Next Generation Science Standards and Related SEL Competencies

Grade	Sample NGSS Performance Expectations	SEL Domains and Competencies
Kindergarten	• Ask questions • Develop and use models • Plan and carry out investigations • Engage in argument from evidence	**Self-awareness:** Developing interests and a sense of purpose **Responsible decision-making:** Demonstrating curiosity and open-mindedness
First Grade	• Plan and carry out investigations • Analyze and interpret data • Construct explanations and design solutions • Obtain, evaluate, and communicate information	**Self-management:** Using planning and organizational skills **Responsible decision-making:** Recognizing how critical thinking skills are useful both inside and outside of school
Second Grade	• Develop and use models • Analyze and interpret data • Construct explanations and design solutions • Engage in argument from evidence	**Relationship skills:** Communicating effectively **Responsible decision-making:** Learning how to make a reasoned judgment after analyzing information, data, and facts
Third Grade	• Define problems • Plan and carry out investigations • Engage in argument from evidence • Obtain, evaluate, and communicate information	**Social:** Communicating and interacting with others **Self-awareness:** Experiencing self-efficacy; developing interests and a sense of purpose

Source: NGSS Lead States. 2013. *Next Generation Science Standards: For States, By States*. Washington, DC: The National Academies Press. Retrieved from www.nextgenscience.org/search-standards

The NGSS standards are also correlated to some of the Common Core Standards for Mathematics and for ELA/Literacy, such as "With prompting and support, ask and answer questions about key details in a text" (K-ESS3–2) and "Participate in shared research and writing projects (e.g., explore a number of books by a favorite author and express opinions about them)" (K-PS3–1), (K-PS3–2), (K-ESS2–1). These ELA standards work beautifully with picture books on any topic and offer opportunities for cross-curricular lessons that address multiple subjects.

Science-themed picture books can be loosely grouped into three categories: fictional stories that use science concepts as plot points within the story; *pourquoi* stories, myths, and legends that offer an array of creative explanations for natural events; and biographies of inspiring figures that feature historical events in STEM fields. The next section will provide examples of each type, with ideas for classroom applications. A full lesson plan and book list are included at the end of the chapter.

Fictional Stories

A variety of picture books weave science themes or examples into the stories' content through the plot, dialogue, and interactions of the characters, which demonstrate key SEL concepts, such as decision-making and problem-solving, and character traits such as kindness, curiosity, grit, resilience, and creativity. One example of a picture book series that weaves science lessons into the characters' dialogue is Geoff Waring's Oscar series (including *Oscar and the Bat: A Book about Sound*; *Oscar and the Moth: A Book About Light*; and *Oscar and the Cricket: A Book About Moving and Rolling*), which is centered around an inquisitive cat who meets other animals that introduce him to scientific concepts. In *Oscar and the Bat*, Oscar's new friend teaches him about how creatures make sounds and how to interpret them: "We make sounds in our throats . . . but some animals talk with different parts of their bodies. When they nest, some male hummingbirds make a loud sound with their wings to warn other birds away. Bottlenose dolphins send messages to one another under water through their blowholes." Oscar demonstrates such SEL traits as curiosity, kindness, perseverance, and decision-making throughout his adventures.

While books like the Oscar series are more directly instructional through the characters' conversations, stories like *Cao Chong Weighs an Elephant* by Songju Ma Daemicke and *Sonya's Chickens* by Phoebe Wahl weave the science concepts into the plot. *Cao Chong* tells the story of the arrival of an elephant to a small village. Amazed by the animal's size, the villagers set out to weigh it but have no scales large enough. Through creative problem-solving that highlights cognitive SEL skills, they come up with a solution using displacement of water to weigh the elephant. *Sonya's Chickens* tells the story of a girl whose beloved baby chick is eaten by a fox. A heartbroken Sonia is comforted by her father, who explains that the fox was feeding its own babies, just as Sonia had fed her chicks. "You did everything you could to make sure your chicks were happy and had full bellies and a warm place to sleep. . . . The fox is no different. He loves his kits too. So even though it's sad for us, we can understand why he did it." Without anthropomorphizing the animals, the story teaches an understanding of the life cycle and food chain and empathy for the animals, which is covered in one of the NGSS standards for third grade, Inheritance and Variation of Traits: Life Cycles and Traits.

Weather events, which are covered in NGSS standards for grades K-3, are highlighted through such picture books as *The Wind Blew* by Pat Hutchins and *Cloudette* by Tom Lichtenheld, which situate the forces of weather as protagonists within the story: "Cloudette was a cloud. A very small cloud. Usually, Cloudette didn't mind being smaller than the average cloud. . . . But once in a while, all the other clouds would run off to do something big and important. Cloudette could see them in the distance, doing all sorts of important cloud things. This made her want to do big and important things, too." As with myths and legends, these stories do not teach the details of the weather patterns and events, but they offer a creative starting place for discussions, lessons, and activities. The SEL themes that can be highlighted include self-awareness by demonstrating empathy and compassion, good decision-making, and facets of identity including healthy self-awareness and self-efficacy. Discussion questions that focus on fictional stories can focus on cognitive skills or the plot points, for example:

- ◆ What emotions did Sonya experience during the story, first when she found that the fox had killed her chick, and then after her father had talked to her?
- ◆ How did Cao Chong and the other villagers show problem-solving skills and critical-thinking skills to solve the challenge of weighing the elephant?
- ◆ How did Cloudette come to find her place in the world?

Pourquoi Stories, Myths, and Legends

Stories from a wide variety of cultures and traditions offer fanciful scenarios and descriptions for natural events such as the changing of the seasons, natural disasters, and astronomical phenomena. A key piece of these stories is a moral or example that involves a character demonstrating or learning an SEL skill such as patience, kindness, resilience, or perspective. Examples of *pourquoi* stories include stories that seek to explain the paths of the sun and moon, such as "Why the Sun and Moon Live in the Sky." In the Nigerian version of the story, the sun and the moon are a married pair who move to the sky to make room for the ocean and his friends, while the Zuni version describes the kidnapping of the sun and the moon by a powerful tribe and their eventual rescue by a pair of friends, a coyote and an eagle. The NGSS standard for Space System ESS1.A: The Universe and its Stars can serve as the core of the lesson, and while the *pourquoi* tales do not provide scientifically accurate details of the solar system, they do offer a lively and engaging starting point to conversations about the cycles of the sun and moon.

The East African creation story "How the Guinea Fowl Got Her Spots" tells the tale of a pair of friends, a golden cow and black guinea fowl, who work together to outwit a hungry lion. As thanks for saving him from the lion, the cow gives the guinea fowl white spots to help camouflage her:

> "Nganga," mooed Coe gratefully, "Twice you have helped me escape from Lion. Now I will help you do the same." Turning around, she dipped her tassled tail into a calabash of milk. Then she shook the tasselful of milk over Guinea Fowl's sleek black feathers—flick, flock, flick—spattering her with creamy white milk. Guinea Fowl craned her head and admired the delicate speckles covering her back....
> "These lovely spots are just the thing for hiding in the shadows and grass!" laughed Nganga.

The story demonstrates SEL competencies such as compassion, showing concern for others' feelings, understanding and expressing gratitude, and good decision-making in outwitting the lion. Creation tales such as these offer excellent opportunities for children to reflect on the motivations and emotions of the characters in the story with questions such as, "How was the character feeling at that point? How did they show their feelings? Did they make good decisions?" Individual or small-group activities for the lesson could focus on having the students create a story of their own and present it in drawings, stories, theatrical performances, or in a spoken presentation, individually or as a group. Alternatively, students could retell the story, taking the parts of various characters, as described in the bibliotherapy technique in Chapter 1. Another fun activity to do with *pourquoi* stories is to have the students write their own versions. For younger students, teachers could provide story starters or plot ideas.

Biographies

Stories of the lives and accomplishments of people in STEM fields offer a wonderful opportunity to discover and discuss SEL themes within the context of scientific events and discoveries. The life stories of inventors and explorers offer inspiring examples of creative problem-solving, determination, and perseverance in the face of hardship and failure.

Biographies of ocean explorers and conservationists include *Manfish: A Story of Jacques Cousteau* by Jennifer Berne, a beautifully illustrated story of how Jacques Cousteau developed the tools and skills he needed to explore the depths of the seas and the resulting impact that his work and discoveries have had on our understanding and conservation of the oceans and their populations. A lovely companion book to *Manfish* is *Life in the Ocean: The Story of Oceanographer Sylvia Earle* by Claire A. Nivola, which describes the life and work of marine biologist, oceanographer, and researcher Sylvia Earle, who, like Jacques Cousteau, has been fascinated by the marine life of the oceans and has sought to protect it. *Otis and Will Discover the Deep* by Barb Rosenstock tells the story of the invention of the bathysphere, a diving tank that allowed its inventors, Otis Baron and Will Beebe, to make record-setting dives in the 1930s to explore the ocean depths. The ingenuity, creativity, and bravery shown by Jacques,

Sylvia, Otis, and Will offer many important SEL lessons in conjunction with the details of deep-ocean life and exploration.

A beautiful picture book that addresses the topic of environmental change is *The Tree Lady: The True Story of How One Tree-Loving Woman Changed a City Forever* by H. Joseph Hopkins, which was mentioned in Chapter 4. *Tree Lady* tells the true story of Kate Sessions, who singlehandedly transformed the heart of San Diego from a treeless desert to the lush parkland of Balboa Park. The story describes and provides vibrant illustrations of the horticultural details of the process, including how Kate selected and gathered seedlings that would flourish in the climate and her organization of a movement to plant thousands of trees and plants in time for San Diego's 1915 Panama-California Exposition. Along with the scientific details of how Sessions and her trees transformed the environment, the story also details Sessions' personal life, which is filled with SEL teaching opportunities around the topics of citizenship, values, ethics, perspective, and perseverance. The story is well suited to correlate to the NGSS strand Interdependent Relationships in Ecosystems: Animals, Plants, and Their Environment, which has a learning outcome (K-ESS2–2) that has students demonstrate understanding by constructing "an argument supported by evidence for how plants and animals (including humans) can change the environment to meet their needs."

An exercise that calls on the students to work on SEL skills related to this could have them draw a picture of San Diego before and after Kate's efforts then share their drawings with the class. A group discussion could focus on the challenges that Kate faced, identifying the emotions that she felt and discussing how she overcame the challenges to reach such an impressive goal. The idea of such a massive undertaking and transformation could be overwhelming to many children, but bringing it down to the level of a single garden could make it meaningful and manageable. Books such as *The Tree Lady* provide excellent opportunities for cross-curricular lessons as well, pulling in details of environmental movements and science lessons on the plants and flowers and their habitats.

A book at a higher reading level that could be used to differentiate the lesson is *Wangari Maathai: The Woman Who Planted*

Millions of Trees by Franck Prévot, which tells the story of Kenyan political activist and environmentalist Wangari Maathai, who was the first African woman to receive the Nobel Peace Prize. She founded the Green Belt Movement to stop the deforestation of Africa and, like Kate Sessions, led a tree-planting initiative that resulted in a transformation of the native landscape with more than 30 million trees planted. Wangari later joined a movement to establish a democratic government in Kenya. The stories of the two remarkable women's efforts and success, and the social and emotional skills that they used to achieve their accomplishments, provide a powerful way to compare and contrast their experiences and circumstances. A comparison point to highlight is the difference in the circumstances of the two women—where they lived, the challenges they faced, and their impact on their environments. The lesson plan at the end of this chapter focuses on the two books and provides ideas for individual and small-group activities, as well as discussion questions.

Math

The Common Core Standards for Mathematics are broken into two categories: standards for mathematical practice and standards for mathematical content. The standards for practice are based on learning processes and proficiencies that are considered vital for students to achieve, many of which support core SEL domains. Table 5.2 provides examples of correlations between the Common Core standards for math practice and SEL domains that run through the standards and can be incorporated in the lessons and exercises.

Picture books related to math touch on a wide variety of SEL themes through the plots of the stories and in biographies and historical details. Math-focused fiction picture books can be loosely grouped by several broad themes: the concept that math surrounds us in our everyday lives; stories that demonstrate number sense (how many, how much, and comparisons); stories that use numbers as characters that prompt emotional responses; and stories that explain a math concept as part of the plot.

Table 5.2 Sample Common Core Standards for Mathematics and Related SEL Domains

Common Core Standards for Mathematical Practice	SEL Domains
Make sense of problems and persevere in solving them	**Cognitive:** Good decision-making; problem-solving and working through challenges; and learning from failure **Perspectives:** Developing a growth mindset, grit, and perseverance **Self-management:** Setting personal and collective goals; using planning and organizational skills
Construct viable arguments and critique the reasoning of others ... justify conclusions, communicate them to others, and respond to the arguments of others	**Relationship skills:** Communicating effectively; practicing teamwork and collaborative problem-solving **Self-awareness:** Having a growth mindset
Model with mathematics ... apply mathematics to solve problems arising in everyday life, society, and the workplace	**Social awareness:** Recognizing situational demands and opportunities **Responsible decision-making:** Learning how to make a reasoned judgment after analyzing information, data, and facts; identifying solutions for personal and social problems; recognizing how critical thinking skills are useful both inside and outside of school

Source: National Governors Association Center for Best Practices, Council of Chief State School Officers. (2010). *Common Core State Standards: Mathematics Standards.* National Governors Association Center for Best Practices, Council of Chief State School Officers.

Non-fiction math picture books focus on the stories of inspiring figures in the field of mathematics who demonstrated remarkable resilience, creativity, and determination.

Math in Our Everyday Lives

Picture books with the theme that math is all around us serve to highlight math themes ranging from patterns in nature to measurements and comparisons that we make throughout our daily routines and interactions. Orly Rubenstein's TedEd animation, "Why do people get so anxious about math?", describes the common occurrence of math anxiety and stresses the importance of normalizing it by having parents and educators be playful with math and focus on the creative aspects of it. These books show the importance and relevance of math abilities in everyday circumstances, pulling their application from abstract equations into a student's daily applications. One example is *Count on Me* by Miguel Tanco, in which a young girl reflects on the interests of her family (music, biology, and art) and announces that her passion is math—"It's often hidden and I love finding it"— pointing out the shapes on the playground, the mathematical challenge of dividing up a family dinner, and the process of building a paper airplane. She tackles challenges through a combination of such SEL traits as ingenuity, resilience, and an openness and curiosity about the world, demonstrating the joy and omnipresence of math and de-emphasizing math's presence as a stressful challenge.

Picture Books About Number Sense

Beginning picture books introduce the concepts of the linear progression of numbers and ideas of number sense, which are a part of the Common Core Standards for Mathematical Practice in kindergarten that focus on representing, relating, and operating on whole numbers and describing shapes and space. These books look at questions of quantities and measurements, providing examples and comparisons in real life. Annie Watson's *Is 2 a Lot?* teaches number sense and linear progression through hilarious comparisons that are answers to a child's question, "Is two a lot?", during a car trip. "Two is not a lot of pennies, but two is a lot of smelly skunks. . . . Ten is not a lot of pieces of popcorn, but it is a lot of chomping dinosaurs . . . One thousand is not a lot of grains of sand, but one thousand is a lot of hot air balloons." The illustrations show the mom and son collecting the numbered objects as they drive along, with the final spread showing a car packed with cowboys, dogs, dinosaurs, knights, and other colorful figures.

Books with scientific statistics that demonstrate number sense, asking "How much?" and "How many?", include Seth Fishman's *A Hundred Billion Trillion Stars*, which quantifies enormous groups of objects on Earth and in our solar system, from the three trillion trees on Earth to the seven billion five hundred million humans, who collectively "weigh about the same as ten quadrillion ants." Lola Schaefer's *Lifetime: The Amazing Numbers in Animal Lives* begins with a single "papery egg sac" that is a spider's lifetime creation and increases in numbers through the 30 roosting holes a woodpecker will drill, up to the 1,000 "teeny-weeny, squiggly-wiggly baby seahorses" that a male seahorse will carry and birth in his lifetime. As with *Count on Me*, these books bring a sense of positivity, curiosity, and ingenuity to the discussion of math, normalizing it for the children. Classroom exercises can extend the concept of the book by numbering collections of items—in the classroom, on the playground, at home, or in thinking about situations in the world at large. A key SEL domain that fits into these books are the idea of identity and sense of place in the world, a fostering of a natural curiosity about math that strips away some of the anxiety around the subject, and a re-emphasis on building cognitive skills and academic self-confidence that will come with math success.

Fictional stories that incorporate number sense and linear progression include *Counting Chickens* by Polly Alakija, which counts animal babies and hens eggs in a village; *Zero Is the Leaves on the Tree* by Betsy Franco, which is a poetic reflection on the number zero—"Zero is the ducks on the pond when the air says winter is coming"—and *Infinity and Me* by Kate Hosford, which mulls over the question, "How could I even think about something as big as infinity?" and answers it with a variety of ideas—infinity is generations of family, a loop of music, and a boundless love for a grandmother. Other books in this category play with the themes of shape, including *A Trapezoid Is Not a Dinosaur!* by Suzanne Morris, which is the story of a group of shapes jockeying for parts in a school play about space; trapezoid's odd shape makes him unsuitable for many traditional roles in the play, and he is encouraged to take the part of a dinosaur; the trapezoid suggests he take the role of a rocket booster, making him "a supportive shape." Mac Barnett and Jon Klassen's shape series that comprises *Square, Circle,* and *Triangle* are stories of shapes interacting in situations that highlight and compare their shapes, while playing and interacting like children. The books have the dry humor shared by many of Barnett and Klassen's books that will appeal to older children and adults as well. *Round* by Joyce Sidman is a meditation on the beauty and purpose of round objects, "I love when round things pop up quickly . . . and last only a moment. Or spin together slowly . . . and last billions of years. Or show themselves night after night, rounder and rounder, until the whole sky holds its breath." These reflections on the omnipresence of mathematical shapes in the world share themes with books like *Count on Me* that highlight and normalize the presence of math concepts in everyday life.

Math Books With Number Protagonists

A common theme in math-related picture books that ties into SEL topics is making numbers into characters in the story, setting them up as protagonists who experience and solve problems through ingenuity, kindness, and other SEL domains. Ayano Imai's *The 108th Sheep* tells the story of a sleepless girl counting sheep, up to the 108th sheep, which lands with a thump, unable to clear the headboard. The ingenuity and support of the other sheep help the 108th on its way and send them all into a deep sleep. Kathryn Otoshi's books *Zero*, *One*, and *Two* give voice to the emotions of the smallest numbers. *Zero* tells of the number's low sense of self-worth in relation to the other numbers, until it realizes that it can exponentially increase the value of its friends by joining them, turning 1 into 1,000,000. Otoshi's award-winning *One* tells the stories of colors and their corresponding emotions ("Blue was a quiet color"), which take on the shape of numbers to counter the anger of red. These books give a sense of whimsy to the linear progression of counting and are excellent starting points for discussions of SEL themes particular to the books, such as social awareness (helping others) in *The 108th Sheep* or relationship skills (demonstrating positive relationships) in *Zero*.

Stories that use math as parts of the plot include *Who Eats First?* by Ae-hae Yoon, which plays on comparisons by telling the story of animals who claim the right to the first bite of a big, juicy peach based on their relative height, weight, and size. The caterpillar outwits the other animals and claims the prize: "If we measure from the shortest to the tallest animal, I'm first. Or from the lightest to the heaviest, I'm first again! Measuring from the shortest ears to the longest . . . well, I have no ears, which makes me number one!" Myths and folktales that incorporate counting include *Two of Everything: A Chinese Folktale* by Lily Toy Hong, which tells the tale of the elderly Haktak couple, who dig up a magical pot that doubles everything put inside. They are delighted by their resulting riches but find themselves in a difficult situation when they fall in the pot and create their own twins. SEL themes addressed in these books include good decision-making (and the impact of good and poor decisions), as well as cognitive skills, problem-solving, and working through challenges.

Biographies and Non-Fiction Histories

The last category of math-related picture books includes biographies and non-fiction histories. Recent books highlight the achievements of women and other minoritized groups who have achieved greatness in the field of math. *The Girl with a Mind for Math: The Story of Raye Montague* by Julia Finley Mosca tells the story in rhyme of Raye Montague, an African-American naval engineer inspired as a child to become an engineer after touring a captured German submarine. Denied entrance into the engineering program because of her race, Raye studied computers and engineering on the side and was the first person to design a naval ship using a computer. *Maryam's Magic: The Story of Mathematician Maryam Mirzakhani* by Megan Reid tells the bittersweet story of the Iranian mathematician Maryam Mirzakhani, the only woman who has won the Fields Medal, the highest honor in the field of math, for her "magic wand theorem" of geometry. Maryam's distinguished career and contributions to the field were marked by extraordinary determination and a growth mindset and were sadly cut short when she died of cancer at the age of 40. *Nothing Stopped Sophie: The Story of Unshakable Mathematician Sophie Germain* by Cheryl Bardoe tells the story of a French woman who lived in the late 18th and early 19th centuries, teaching herself math during the French Revolution and attending classes under the pseudonym Monsieur LeBlanc. "In 1816, Sophie Germain became the first woman to win a grand prize from the Royal Academy of Sciences. . . .' The human spirit,' she later reflected, 'requires more resources inside when outside it has less.'" The stories of the obstacles that all of these women faced and overcame serve as great discussion starters on how to foster the skills that students need to succeed in math, but they also offer examples of successful women in the field and the SEL skills they needed to succeed, such as grit, resilience, overcoming failure and obstacles, and problem-solving.

Technology

The International Society for Technology in Education (ISTE) offers technology standards for students in K-12. Table 5.3 lists the seven broad categories of standards with examples of specific outcomes and correlated SEL themes and domains.

Table 5.3 Sample Standards for Technology and Related SEL Domains

ISTE Standard	Sample Outcomes	SEL Domains and Competencies
Empowered Learner	Students articulate and set personal learning goals, develop strategies leveraging technology to achieve them, and reflect on the learning process itself to improve learning outcomes. Students use technology to seek feedback that informs and improves their practice.	**Cognitive:** Good decision-making; problem-solving and working through challenges; and learning from failure **Self-management:** Goal-setting, using planning and organizational skills
Digital Citizen	Students cultivate and manage their digital identity and reputation and are aware of the permanence of their actions in the digital world. Students engage in positive, safe, legal and ethical behavior when using technology. Students demonstrate an understanding of and respect for the rights and obligations of using and sharing intellectual property.	**Values:** Ethical values, character traits, and habits that position a child to be a compassionate person who contributes to their community and world in positive ways **Identity:** Healthy self-awareness, self-efficacy, and sense of identity and place in the world

(Continued)

Table 5.3 (Continued)

ISTE Standard	Sample Outcomes	SEL Domains and Competencies
Knowledge Constructor	Students build knowledge by actively exploring real-world issues and problems, developing ideas and theories, and pursuing answers and solutions.	**Social awareness:** Recognizing situational demands and opportunities; understanding the influences of organizations and systems on behavior **Responsible decision-making:** Identifying solutions for personal and social problems; recognizing how critical thinking skills are useful both inside and outside of school
Innovative Designer	Students exhibit a tolerance for ambiguity, perseverance, and the capacity to work with open-ended problems.	**Perspectives:** Developing a growth mindset, grit, and perseverance **Self-awareness:** Having a growth mindset; developing interests and a sense of purpose
Global Collaborator	Students use digital tools to connect with learners from a variety of backgrounds and cultures, engaging with them in ways that broaden mutual understanding and learning. Students use collaborative technologies to work with others, including peers, experts, or community members, to examine issues and problems from multiple viewpoints. Students contribute constructively to project teams, assuming various roles and responsibilities to work effectively toward a common goal. Students explore local and global issues and use collaborative technologies to work with others to investigate solutions.	**Social:** Communicating, playing, and interacting with others, and managing conflicts **Relationship skills:** Practicing teamwork and collaborative problem-solving; communicating effectively **Identity:** Fostering an understanding of the diversity of identities within local and global communities

Source: International Society for Technology in Education. (2000). ISTE National Educational Technology Standards (NETS). Eugene, OR. Retrieved from www.iste.org/standards/iste-standards-for-students

Picture books that focus on technology often have themes of creativity, ingenuity, and problem-solving along with cognitive skills, such as task planning and initiation, time management, and good decision-making and communication skills. These books tie in well with maker-space lessons with open-ended creativity questions, problem-solving projects, and collaborative inventions. *Not a Box* by Antoinette Portis has minimal words but vivid pictures that help kids imagine beyond a simple object—the box can be a robot, the basket of a hot air balloon, or a rocket. A book that addresses the joy of creative construction along with the pain of peer rejection is *The Little Red Fort* by Brenda Maier, which tells the story of a girl inspired to build; she asks her brothers to help at various stages and they refuse, but she perseveres. When she finishes the fort and declares that she will enjoy it by herself, the brothers pitch in to finish it, and all the siblings enjoy a "fort-warming party."

Many picture books have SEL themes of overcoming obstacles, criticism, and failures. Examples include *The Most Magnificent Thing* by Ashley Spires, which tells the story of a girl creating the magnificent object she has in her imagination, through many false starts and failures. A companion story is *What Do You Do with an Idea?* by Kobi Yamada, which tells the story of a child with an idea that becomes a companion:

> It grew bigger. And we became friends. I showed it to other people even though I was afraid of what they would say. I was afraid that it people saw it, they would laugh at it. I was afraid they would think it was silly. And many of them did. They said it was no good. They said it was too weird.

The beauty of the idea was in its uniqueness and its importance, and at the end of the book the child comes to the realization that with an idea you change the world. *The Most Magnificent Thing* and *What Do You Do with an Idea?*, like the math picture books, inspire children to imagine what they can do without the anxiety and stress of intrinsic and extrinsic pressures around success. These books, with beautiful illustrations and inspiring text, foster the SEL skills that students need to enter and succeed in STEM subjects: creativity and inspiration; task initiation and planning; problem-solving, working through challenges, and learning from failure; and nurturing optimism, a growth mindset, grit, and perseverance. They are an excellent starting point for a hands-on lesson that includes small-group activities or challenges, such as having students build the longest string of chains made from a single pieces of paper or using cardboard to build the tallest or strongest structure.

Biographies within the technology theme include *Grace Hopper: Queen of Computer Code* by Laurie Wallmark, which tells the story of the groundbreaking computer coder and inventor Grace Hopper, who enrolled in the Navy to help write computer programs for the earliest computers. Forced to initially retire at age 60, she convinced the Navy to recall her to active duty, where she served until her retirement at the age of 79. The story is beautifully illustrated and includes humorous and engaging stories of Grace's life and career—including the time she fixed a computer by removing a moth that was blocking a circuit and then coined the term "computer bug."

Chris Barton's *Whoosh! Lonnie Johnson's Super-Soaking Stream of Inventions* tells the story of an African American NASA engineer who comes up with the idea of a massive water gun and works through many obstacles to find backers and buyers. Lonnie's story touches on many cognitive SEL themes, from problem-solving to overcoming failure and developing grit and resilience.

A lesson that combines the creativity, construction, and inventions of technology with the core domains of SEL has students start with a main story about the life and accomplishments of a ground-breaking figure in technology. Initial discussion questions can focus on the obstacles they faced, the steps they took to overcome them, and the outcome and its role in the world. The students then work individually or in small groups on an invention of their own, starting with making an explanation of how it would work and what problem it would solve. Idea prompts can be shared with the younger children or those who need a starting place. Fostering task initiation and planning, the students can think of the tools and materials they need and make a blueprint with illustrations, instructions, and a plan for how to create the invention. As a large group the students can come back together and share their ideas, discussing what their challenges were and comparing the processes and final outcomes.

Though the subjects of STEM seem at first to be too technical to fit easily into picture books with SEL focuses, the core topics of the books dovetail well with many SEL domains. Scientific explanations, challenges, and discoveries are woven through many picture books, whether they are topic-specific, such as the Oscar series, or beloved tales and myths that address questions in nature, measurements, comparisons, and other mathematical or scientific themes. The most powerful lessons that can be taught with these texts focus on creativity, overcoming adversity and facing failures, and nurturing cognitive skills, which are vital for fostering success and joy in pursuing STEM classes and careers.

LESSON PLAN

Title and Grade
The Tree Planters: How Two Inspiring Women Improved Our Planet Grades: 1–3
Standards and Learning Objectives
Next Generation Science Standards • 2-LS4–1. Make observations of plants and animals to compare the diversity of life in different habitats. • 3-LS4–4. Make a claim about the merit of a solution to a problem caused when the environment changes and the types of plants and animals that live there may change. **C3 Framework Standards: Geography** • D2.Geo.5.K-2. Describe how human activities affect the cultural and environmental characteristics of places or regions. • D2.Geo.6.K-2. Identify some cultural and environmental characteristics of specific places.

Common Core Standards for ELA: Literature
- RL.2.1. Ask and answer such questions as who, what, where, when, why, and how to demonstrate understanding of key details in a text.

Common Core Standards for ELA: Informational Text
- RI.2.3. Describe the connection between a series of historical events, scientific ideas or concepts, or steps in technical procedures in a text.
- RI.2.9. Compare and contrast the most important points presented by two texts on the same topic.

Common Core Standards for ELA: Speaking and Listening
- SL.2.2. Recount or describe key ideas or details from a text read aloud or information presented orally or through other media.

SEL Standard: CASEL
- Responsible decision-making: The abilities to make caring and constructive choices about personal behavior and social interactions across diverse situations

SEL Standards: Harvard
- Cognitive: Problem-solving, working through challenges, task initiation and task management
- Values: Being a compassionate person who contributes to their community and world in positive ways
- Identity: Fostering an understanding of the diversity of identities within local and global communities

Learning Objectives
After reading two texts on prominent environmentalists with similar goals, the students will compare and contrast the experiences, circumstance, and actions of these people, through individual and small-group final projects.

ASSESSMENT
Informal assessment will include assessment of students' participation in whole- and small-group discussions and completion of the daily activities. Assessments will vary

based on the level of the students; a suggested differentiated assessment would be:

- **Level 1:** Students will focus on *The Tree Lady*, with additional support as needed for understanding vocabulary and themes. Students will identify key details from the text (character, setting, plot details) and will be able to make basic comparisons between the two texts in discussion. They will be able to discuss how ecosystems differ and what that means for the types of plants and animals that live there, and they will be able to describe the impact of Kate's work on San Diego.

- **Level 2:** Students will focus on either book, as appropriate to their reading levels. They will use context clues to determine meanings of words or phrases and will be able to show understanding of sequence, cause and effect, and literary elements, such as character and setting. They will be able to offer comparisons between the texts in discussion. Students will be able to discuss content specifics, including the location, ecosystems, and challenges of Wangari and Kate. What steps did they take to accomplish their goals, and did they succeed?

- **Level 3:** Students will focus on *Wangari Maathai*. They will be able to provide evidence when responding to questions/making inferences, discuss consequences and implications, and compare and contrast themes and concepts between the two texts, both in the areas of the protagonists' actions, challenges, and responses and in comparison of the two ecosystems. The discussion should include more in-depth details of the obstacles (political and social) that Wangari and Kate faced and how they overcame them.

LEARNING PLAN

Instructional Resources and Materials

- *The Tree Lady: The True Story of How One Tree-Loving Woman Changed a City Forever* by H. Joseph Hopkins

- *Wangari Maathai: The Woman Who Planted a Million Trees* by Franck Prévot
- Pre-assessment (optional)
- K/W/L chart
- Story sections and vocabulary matching worksheet
- Additional books and/or links to videos
- Butcher paper or large sheets of paper for a mural or multi-paneled picture
- Presentation medium, as available: paper, computer with PowerPoint, audio or video recording hardware
- Research materials

Daily Plans

Stage 1: Group Activity (1 Day)
Pre-assessment (Optional: Use results of pre-assessment to assign individual activities.)
- Pre-test vocabulary from each book—individually or in a group setting.
- **Vocabulary**:
  - *Level 1*: environment, ecosystem, nursery, desert
  - *Level 2*: colonists, independence, cultivate, plantation
- Have students complete the K,W of a K/W/L chart individually; roll them into a class-wide K and W, and discuss. Questions:
  - Where are San Diego, California, and Kenya?
  - What is an ecosystem?
  - Why are trees important?

Begin with a reading of one of the following books:
- *Tell Me, Tree: All About Trees for Kids* by Gail Gibbons
- *The Lorax* by Dr. Seuss
- *The Magic and Mystery of Trees* by Jen Green

After completing the introductory discussion, ask small groups of children to think about the roles that trees play in our environment and world.
- How do we use trees?
- What happens when trees are cut down?
- What happens when trees are replanted?
- What does an environmentalist do?

Stage 2: Read Aloud and Activities (2 Days)
Read aloud either *The Tree Lady: The True Story of How One Tree-Loving Woman Changed a City Forever* or *Wangari Maathai: The Woman Who Planted a Million Trees* by Franck Prévot. Using the CROWD strategy described in Chapter 4, or another format to guide your development of discussion questions, ask students a variety of questions that allow them to develop their understanding of the key points in the text, including those that are directly stated and those that must be inferred.

- **Completion:** Kate Sessions/Wangari Maathai was concerned about _____.
- **Recall:** How did Kate/Wangari make the decision to plant trees?
- **Open-ended:** What kind of skills did Kate/Wangari need to get their education and begin their tree-planting campaigns?
- **W's:** Who influenced Kate/Wangari's views? What was the impact or result of their tree-planting efforts? Where did Kate/Wangari do their work? When did they live? Why did Kate leave her job as a teacher/Why did Wangari join a political movement?
- **Distancing:** What have you heard about in the news regarding environmental or conservation efforts? What others books have we read that show people trying to make a difference in environmental ways? What are some things you could do to help environmental conservation?

On the second day of this stage, small groups of students will read the book they haven't read yet—either *The Tree Lady: The True Story of How One Tree-Loving Woman Changed a City Forever* or *Wangari Maathai: The Woman Who Planted a Million Trees*. If needed, students can work with the teacher or teaching assistant, or they can listen to an audio version of the story. They can either be given a piece of paper to document their thinking, or they can discuss and share their discussion with the whole class. Questions could include:

- What was the problem Kate/Wangari was trying to address? How were their problems similar? Different?

- What were some of the steps they took to reach their goals?
- What challenges did they meet, and how were they similar or different to the other person's? How did they respond to those challenges?
- What were the results of their efforts? How were they similar? different?

Stage 3: Differentiated Learning (3–4 Days—1½ Days per Project)
Learners' individual needs will be met through differentiation of content, process, and product. Activities can be individually focused or completed in small groups.

Group Projects:
1. At least one team will work on each book. Students will draw a mural or multi-paneled picture showing the story arc, characters, and settings. They will discuss as a whole group the similarities and differences between the two books, including the settings, the main characters, their emotions and actions, and the plots.
2. Using information from the texts and with additional assistance as needed, students in teams will research the ecosystems of San Diego and Kenya. Each team will create a presentation in the form of a drawing, spoken presentation, or PowerPoint. They will present and discuss the similarities and differences of the ecosystems.
3. Using the information in each book and extra research materials as needed, each team will learn about the lives of the two women, create a presentation with multimedia, and present to the group. Students will discuss the similarities and differences between the two women as a whole group.

Individual Activities:
Level 1: Students will identify key characters in the book, putting the story pieces in order and matching vocabulary to

meanings. They will describe on audio or video three similarities and differences between characters. (Use this opportunity to teach the technology skills needed as well: basic audio/video recording.)

Level 2: Create a timeline that includes at least five specific events from the book, as well as five additional events about the region or on a related theme during the same period.

Level 3: Research and write a biography of another inspiring environmentalist or women's rights figure. Compare the biographical details with those of the original book.

Stage 4: Revisit Group Activity (1 Day)
On the first day, students were introduced to themes of ecosystem and environmental activism. On this final day, students can reflect back on two aspects of the lesson: the lives and impacts of Kate and Wangari and a discussion of ecosystems and the role of trees. Go back to the KWL chart and fill in key points of the lesson.

- The lives and actions of Kate and Wangari: Reflect on the projects that Kate and Wangari undertook, as well as the social and emotional skills that they used, giving examples of such skills from problem-solving and decision-making to grit, overcoming failure, and resilience, and describing the impact of their efforts. The discussion can focus as well on how much they did as individuals and stress the impact that each and every one of us can have in helping the environment.

- Ecosystems and the role of trees: Discuss the definition of an ecosystem and the role of trees in our world, thinking back to the first books that were read and the details of the importance of trees in Kate and Wangari's lives and to everyone on Earth. Discuss how we can all save (and even replant trees).

> **References**
>
> Gibbons, G. (2002). *Tell me, tree: All about trees for kids*. Little Brown.
> Green, J. (2019). *The magic and mystery of trees* (C. McElfatrick, Illus.) DK Children.
> Hopkins, H. J. (2013). *The tree lady: The true story of how one tree-loving woman changed a city forever* (J. McElmurry, Illus.). Simon & Schuster.
> Prévot, F. (2015). *Wangari Maathai: The woman who planted millions of trees* (A. Fronty, Illus.) Charlesbridge.
> Seuss, D. (1971). *The Lorax*. Random House Books.
> Winter, J. (2008). *Wangari's trees of peace: A true story from Africa*. Harcourt Children's Books.

References

Chen, Y. S. (2013). *The primeval flood catastrophe: Origins and early development in Mesopotamian traditions*. Oxford University Press.

Dundes, A. (1988). *The flood myth*. University of California Press.

Frazer, J. G. (2013). *The great flood*. Jason Colavito.

Gibbons, G. (2002). *Tell me, tree: All about trees for kids* (Illustrated edition). Little Brown.

Green, J. (2019). *The magic and mystery of trees* (Illustrated edition). DK Children.

Gunderson, E. A., Park, D., Maloney, E. A., Beilock, S. L., & Levine, S. C. (2018). Reciprocal relations among motivational frameworks, math anxiety, and math achievement in early elementary school. *Journal of Cognition and Development, 19*(1), 21–46.

International Society for Technology in Education. (2000). *ISTE national educational technology standards (NETS)*. Eugene, OR. www.iste.org/standards/iste-standards-for-students

Kaminski, J. A., & Sloutsky, V. M. (2020). The use and effectiveness of colorful, contextualized, student-made material for elementary mathematics instruction. *International Journal of STEM Education, 7*(1), 1–23.

Kaminski, J. A., Sloutsky, V. M., & Heckler, A. F. (2008). The advantage of abstract examples in learning math. *Science, 320*, 454–455.

National Governors Association Center for Best Practices, Council of Chief State School Officers. (2010). *Common core state standards: Mathematics standards*. National Governors Association Center for Best Practices, Council of Chief State School Officers.

NGSS Lead States. (2013). *Next generation science standards: For states, by states*. The National Academies Press. www.nextgenscience.org/search-standards

Ramirez, G., Shaw, S. T., & Maloney, E. A. (2018). Math anxiety: Past research, promising interventions, and a new interpretation framework. *Educational Psychologist, 53*(3), 145–164.

Seuss, D. (1971). *The lorax*. Random House Books for Young Readers.

van Veelen, R., Derks, B., & Endedijk, M. D. (2019). Double trouble: How being outnumbered and negatively stereotyped threatens career outcomes of women in STEM. *Frontiers in Psychology, 10*. https://doi.org/10.3389/fpsyg.2019.00150

Wieselmann, J. R., Roehrig, G. H., & Kim, J. N. (2020). Who succeeds in STEM? Elementary girls' attitudes and beliefs about self and STEM. *School Science and Mathematics, 120*(5), 297–308.

Zewe, A. (2021, July 9). Can machine learning bring more diversity to STEM? *Harvard John A. Paulson School of Engineering and Applied Sciences*. www.seas.harvard.edu/news/2021/07/can-machine-learning-bring-more-diversity-stem.

Book List

Science

Alakija, P. (2014). *Counting chickens*. Frances Lincoln Children's Bks.

Berne, J. (2008). *Manfish: A story of Jacques Cousteau* (E. Puybaret, Illus.). Chronicle Books.

Burleigh, R. (2013). *Look up!: Henrietta Leavitt, pioneering woman astronomer* (R. Colón, Illus.). Simon & Schuster/Paula Wiseman Books.

Hopkins, H. J. (2013). *The tree lady: The true story of how one tree-loving woman changed a city forever* (J. McElmurry, Illus.). Beach Lane Books.

Hutchins, P. (1993). *The wind blew*. Aladdin.

Keating, J. (2017). *Shark lady: The true story of how Eugenie Clark became the ocean's most fearless scientist* (H. Robidoux, Illus.). Sourcebooks Explore.

Knutson, B. (1990). *How the guinea fowl got her spots: A Swahili tale of friendship*. Carolrhoda Books.

Lichtenheld, T. (2011). *Cloudette*. Henry Holt and Co.

Marinov, I. (2021). *The boy whose head was filled with stars: A life of Edwin Hubble* (D. Marcero, Illus.). Enchanted Lion Books.

Nivola, C. A. (2012). *Life in the ocean: The story of oceanographer Sylvia Earle*. Farrar, Straus and Giroux.

Prevot, F. (2015). *Wangari Maathai: The woman who planted millions of trees* (A. Fronty, 2015). Charlesbridge.

Robeson, T. (2019). *Queen of physics: How Wu Chien Shiung helped unlock the secrets of the atom* (R. Huang, Illus.). Sterling Children's Books.

Rosenstock, B. (2018). *Otis and will discover the deep: The record-setting dive of the Bathysphere* (K. Roy, Illus.). Little, Brown Books for Young Readers.

Soundar, C. (2017). *Pattan's pumpkin: An Indian flood story* (F. Lessac, Illus.). Candlewick.

Wahl, P. (2018). *Sonya's chickens*. Tundra Books.

Wallmark, L. (2017). *Grace Hopper: Queen of computer code* (K. Wu, Illus.). Sterling Children's Books.

Waring, G. (2009). *Oscar and the bat: A book about sound*. Candlewick.

Winter, J. (2017). *The world is not a rectangle: A portrait of architect Zaha Hadid*. Beach Lane Books.

Math

Arihara, B. F. S. (2009). *Zero is the leaves on the trees* (S. Arihara, Illus.). Scholastic.

Bardoe, C. (2018). *Nothing stopped Sophie: The story of unshakable mathematician Sophie Germain* (B. McClintock, Illus.). Little, Brown Books for Young Readers.

Barnett, M. (2017). *Triangle* (J. Klassen, Illus.). Candlewick.

Barnett, M. (2018). *Square* (J. Klassen, Illus.). Candlewick.

Barnett, M. (2019). *Circle* (J. Klassen, Illus.). Candlewick.

Daemicke, S. M. (2017). *Cao Chong weighs an elephant* (C. Wald, Illus.). Arbordale Publishing.

Fishman, S. (2020). *A hundred billion trillion stars* (I. Greenberg, Illus.). Greenwillow Books.

Hong, L. T. (2017). *Two of everything*. Albert Whitman & Company.

Hosford, K. (2012). *Infinity and me* (G. Swiatkowska, Illus.). Carolrhoda Books.

Imai, A. (2007). *The 108th sheep*. Tiger Tales.
McElligott, M. (2003). *The lion's share: A tale of halving cake and eating it, too*. Scholastic.
Morris, S. (2019). *A trapezoid is not a dinosaur!* Charlesbridge.
Mosca, J. F. (2020). *The girl with a mind for math: The story of Raye Montague* (J. Rieley, Illus.). The Innovation Press.
Otoshi, K. (2008). *One*. KO Kids Books.
Otoshi, K. (2010). *Zero*. KO Kids Books.
Otoshi, K. (2014). *Two*. KO Kids Books.
Reid, M. (2021). *Maryam's magic: The story of mathematician Maryam Mirzakhani* (A. Jaleel, Illus.). Balzer + Bray.
Schaefer, L. M. (2016). *Lifetime: The amazing numbers in animal lives* (C. S. Neal). Chronicle Books.
Sidman, J. (2017). *Round* (T. Yoo, Illus.). Clarion Books.
Tanco, M. (2019). *Count on me*. Tundra Books.
Watson, A. (2021). *Is 2 a lot?* (R. Evans, Illus.). Tilbury House Publishers.
Yoon, A. (2015). *Who eats first?* (H. Yang, Illus.). Tantan Publishing.

Technology
Adamson, G. (2018). *Douglas, You're a genius!* Schwartz & Wade.
Barton, C. (2016). *Whoosh!: Lonnie Johnson's super-soaking stream of inventions* (D. Tate, Illus.). Charlesbridge.
Beaty, A. (2013). *Rosie Revere, engineer* (D. Roberts, Illus.). Abrams Books for Young Readers.
Beaty, A. (2019). *Rosa Pionera, ingeniera* (D. Roberts, Illus.). Beascoa.
Maier, B. (2018a). *The little red fort* (S. Sánchez, Illus.). Scholastic Press.
Maier, B. (2018b). *El fuertecito rojo* (S. Sánchez, Illus.). Scholastic en español.
Portis, A. (2006). *Not a box*. HarperCollins.
Spires, A. (2013). *The most magnificent thing*. Kids Can Press.
Yamada, K. (2014). *What do you do with an idea?* Compendium Inc.

6

Integrating SEL and Social Studies Using Picture Books

Children are born with a sense of empathy towards others, demonstrated by the fact that even newborn babies can react to other infants' distress (Walsh & Walsh, 2019). A variety of environmental and social factors influence the development of empathy skills from childhood into adolescence, including appropriate support by parents and caregivers and children's emotional regulation and socialization at home and in school (Ornaghi, Conte, & Grazzani, 2020; Spinrad & Gal, 2018). The development of both empathy and perspective-taking opens the way to increasing prosocial behaviors such as cooperation and sharing, and reducing aggression, bullying, and social prejudice (Aslan & Köksal Akyol, 2020; Eisenberg, Eggum, & Di Giunta, 2010; Feshbach & Feshbach, 2009). Empathy is a key component of social and emotional learning, and the development of empathy and perspective-taking supports many other SEL skills, including social awareness, self-awareness, self-management, and good decision-making.

The topics covered in elementary-grade social studies courses are deeply rooted in themes of empathy, perspective, and identity, resulting in a natural link between teaching the subject content along with SEL competencies. As students learn about the people and events within their social studies curriculum, key questions can be starting points for students to consider and discuss the motivations and impacts of the people and events:

- "How and why did those events come to pass?" and "How and why did the person/people do what they did?"
- "What impact did the people or events have?"
- "What would the world be like today if those people had not existed or those events had not taken place?"

These three questions set up discussions around the origins, motivations, and consequences of people's decisions and actions, and help students see the impacts of people's actions, whether they are sparks that ignite massive movements for change or small acts of kindness. From there, the lessons and discussions can flow into all areas of social and emotional learning, from such cognitive skills as task-planning, problem-solving, and learning from failure to social awareness, self-awareness, and responsible decision-making, among many others.

Picture books in social studies include biographies of historical figures, accounts of historical events, and historical fiction that draw on story lines of people's lives and experiences. These stories pull in aspects of every Harvard SEL competency: cognitive skills, such as task planning and initiation and good decision-making; emotion and social domains, demonstrating how people throughout history managed their emotions, interacted, communicated, and dealt with conflict; values, including developing ethics, character traits, and habits that help the student contribute positively to the local and global communities; and perspectives, such as fostering optimism, courage, determination, perseverance. Aspects of CASEL competencies that are beautifully demonstrated include social awareness skills, such as identifying diverse social norms, recognizing situational demands, and understanding the influences of organizations and systems on behavior, self-awareness, and self-management.

This chapter will discuss how to integrate the key aspects of social studies content with SEL competencies and domains. Both the standards and the content topics within social studies are wide-reaching, touching on themes as diverse as geography, time and change, individual development and identity, science and technology, production and consumption, and civics. The chapter will begin with a summary of the two core sets of standards for social studies, grouping them into five overarching themes, and then examine how each theme can be integrated with SEL domains, with examples of specific stories and associated lesson ideas.

Social Studies standards. There are two key sets of standards for social studies: the National Council for Social Studies (NCSS) standards and the College, Career, and Civic Life (C3) Framework for Social Studies, which was a result of a three-year, state-led collaborative effort. These standards overlap and can be effectively integrated with each other, and they can be correlated to Common Core standards, including the Common Core standards for English Language and Math.

The (NCSS) standards are grouped into ten organizing strands:

- Culture
- Time, continuity, and change
- People, places, and environments
- Individual development and identity
- Individuals, groups, and institutions
- Power, authority, and governance
- Production, distribution, and consumption
- Science, technology, and society
- Global connections
- Civic ideals and practices

The College, Career, and Civic Life (C3) Framework seeks to make students aware of the past and of changing cultural and physical environments. The C3 Framework has four topic-focused subsections: civics, economics, geography, and history. The framework uses an inquiry-based approach that includes four dimensions: developing questions and planning inquiries, applying disciplinary concepts and tools, evaluating sources and using evidence, and communicating conclusions and taking informed action. The C3 standards are designed to have direct connections to the Common Core State Standards for English

Language Arts, providing rich opportunities for cross-curricular lessons and activities.

The C3 Framework and NCSS standards offer a multitude of entry points to social and emotional learning themes. Table 6.1

Table 6.1 Sample Social Studies Standards and Related SEL Competencies

Social Studies Standard	Sample Questions	SEL Domains
C3 Framework: Civics	• Describe democratic principles such as equity, fairness, and respect for legitimate authority and rules. • How can people work together to make decisions in the classroom? • How can we apply civic ideals and practices in home, school, and the community?	**Values:** Understanding traits and habits that contribute to the world in positive ways **Relationship skills:** Developing the capacity to communicate clearly, listen effectively, cooperate, and work collaboratively
C3 Framework: Economics	• Identify the benefits and costs of making various personal decisions. • Explain how scarcity necessitates decision-making. • Describe why people in one country trade goods and services with people in other countries.	**Responsible decision-making:** • Anticipating and evaluating the consequences of one's actions • Reflecting on one's role to promote personal, family, and community well-being • Evaluating personal, interpersonal, community, and institutional impacts
C3 Framework: Geography	• Identify some cultural and environmental characteristics of specific places. • Identify ways that a catastrophic disaster may affect people living in a place.	**Identity:** Identifying one's place in the world and understanding the diversity of identities within local and global communities **Social awareness:** Feeling compassion for others; recognizing family, school, and community resources and supports

(Continued)

Table 6.1 (Continued)

Social Studies Standard	Sample Questions	SEL Domains
C3 Framework: History	• Compare perspectives of people in the past to those of people in the present. • Generate questions about individuals and groups who have shaped a significant historical change.	**Social awareness:** Understanding the perspectives of others, including those from diverse backgrounds, cultures, and contexts **Identity:** Fostering an understanding of the diversity of identities in the world
NCSS Theme: Culture	• How are groups of people alike and different? • How do the beliefs, values, and behaviors of a group of people help the group meet its needs and solve problems?	**Social awareness:** Understanding historical and social norms for behavior **Responsible decision-making:** Evaluating personal, interpersonal, community, and institutional impacts
NCSS Theme: Individual Development and Identity	• How can I learn to cooperate and collaborate with others? • How do choices I make influence who I am and how others see me? • What questions are important to ask about who I am and who I am becoming?	**Cognitive:** Learning good decision-making; problem-solving and working through challenges; learning from failure **Self-awareness:** Understanding one's own emotions, thoughts, and values and how they influence behavior across contexts

Sources: *National curriculum standards for social studies: A framework for teaching, learning, and assessment.* (2010). National Council for the Social Studies (NCSS). Washington, DC. National Council for the Social Studies. (2013). *The college, career, and civic life (C3) framework for social studies state standards: Guidance for enhancing the rigor of k-12 civics, economics, geography, and history.* National Council for the Social Studies (NCSS). Washington, DC.

shows examples of correlating the frameworks and themes with SEL domains. For example, within the C3 subsection of civics, there are rich opportunities to discuss the idea of values in such contexts as the rights and responsibilities of people within a group and applying civic virtues and democratic principles.

Many of the NCSS themes draw on the SEL domain of identity—examining and defining one's own identity within familial, cultural, local, and global settings, and considering similarities and differences with other communities, across locations and time periods. These topics prompt students to examine different perspectives and emotions, including examples of perseverance, optimism, and determination, and to illustrate social skills, including social awareness, good communication, and conflict management.

By integrating the themes and standards of the C3 Framework and the NCSS standards, the topics covered within social studies in grades K-3 can be divided in to five broad categories: civics, community, and government; history; economics; geography; and identity and culture. These categories bring together the core subject content with a wide breadth of SEL domains and competencies and offer many opportunities for pulling in picture books that bridge content and SEL themes.

Civics, Community, and Government

This category includes two NCSS strands (Power, Authority, and Governance, and Civic Ideals and Practices) and standards from the C3 civics dimension. It examines such topics as democratic principles and the rights and responsibilities of citizens and government in a constitutional democracy. Several of the C3 and NCSS standards focus on communities, looking at the roles and responsibilities of people and authorities within a community, how communities accomplish tasks, how people have tried to improve their communities over time, and the process of decision-making within communities and governments.

Lessons around democracy. A large focus within this category is books about the democratic process. Narrative picture books that demonstrate or describe the practices of democracy include *Vote for Our Future!* by Margaret McNamara, which tells the story of the students at a school that is used as a polling place and their campaigns to get out the vote in their community. *What Can A Citizen Do?* by Dave Eggers has large, bold illustrations and minimal text but beautifully gets across a citizen's roles and responsibilities and the impact that a single person can make:

> A citizen is just like you
> A citizen can plant a tree
> A citizen can help a neighbor
> A citizen can join a cause

The text closes with "Everything makes an impact on a bigger big than you. And it all starts with the question: What can a citizen do?" The call for participation within the democratic process is shared in *Equity's Call: The Story of Voting Rights* by Deborah Diesen, which tells the historical story of the voting process in the United States, beginning with the country's founders and following through the universal suffrage movements, ending with a similar call for everyone to vote.

A lesson that ties in with these themes and books can focus on the shared responsibility, roles, and decision-making processes within the classroom or the school, such as selecting the class activities or books for the day/week, electing a mascot or team name for the room, or distributing responsibilities among the groups in the classroom. Alternatively, students can discuss an issue within the local, national, or global community, such as drives to recycle and to clean up the community or to collect food, clothing, or books for those in need.

This exercise draws on a variety of SEL skills, including cognitive tasks, such as executive functioning skills; social skills, such as good communication and conflict management; features of values and identity domains; and aspects of the CASEL competencies of self-awareness, social awareness, and responsible decision-making. On the curriculum side, this lesson addresses questions from the NCSS standards, including:

- ◆ What are the rights and responsibilities of people in a group?
- ◆ What are power and authority?
- ◆ What are civic ideals?
- ◆ How can we become informed and engage in meaningful civic action?

This topic correlates closely to several dimensions within the C3 Framework, such as:

- Describes roles and responsibilities of people in authority (D2.Civ.1.K-2)
- Explain how all people, not just official leaders, play important roles in a community (D2.Civ.2.K-2)
- Describe how communities work to accomplish tasks, establish responsibilities, and fulfill roles of authority (D2.Civ.6.K-2)
- Explain how a democracy relies on people's responsible participation, and draw implications for how individuals should participate (D2.Civ.2.3–5)

Lessons about community. The second broad example of themes and picture books in this category is the topic of community, which is beautifully addressed in picture books such as *Last Stop on Market Street*, originally referenced in Chapter 4, and *Hey Wall: A Story of Art and Community* by Susan Verde, which is the story of a large, unpainted wall in a community that has grown cracked and ugly over time ("No one looks up at you. There is nothing to cheer for. You are only lonely concrete."). The community comes together and paints a huge, colorful mural on the wall that represents the people and places of the community ("Look at you now. You are beautiful! Now you tell the *real* story of us. And together *we* are somethin' to see!"). Many of the books that fall into the category of identity and culture, described later in this chapter, are also an excellent fit with the theme of community.

The NCSS theme of individual development and identity calls on students to be able to explore factors of personal identity, including "physical attribute, gender, race, and culture." That theme has a strand for early elementary grades: "[Y]oung learners develop their personal identities in the context of families, peers, schools, and communities. Central to this development are the exploration, identification, and analysis of how individuals and groups are alike and how they are unique, as well as how they relate to each other in supportive and collaborative ways" (NCSS, 2010). *Last Stop on Market Street* ties into the NCSS culture theme's questions for exploration, including "How are groups of people alike and different?" and "What is cultural diversity, and how does diversity develop both within and across cultures?" The book also ties into multiple C3 Framework dimensions, such as the dimension of geographic representations, which includes several opportunities for creating maps and geographical representations, for example, "Use maps, globes, and other simple geographic models to identify cultural and environmental characteristics of places" (D2.Geo.3.K-2).

The NCSS strands and the C3 dimensions can be addressed through the plot, dialogue, and images from *Last Stop on Market Street*. A small-group activity based on *Last Stop on Market Street* could involve students working together on drawing the route that CJ and Nana take home on the bus, noting the buildings, stops, and people they see along the way. In conjunction with that exercise, students can draw a map of their own community, the area of the school, or their own neighborhood, noting similarities and differences with the route of Market Street. While addressing the specific content standard, this exercise also pulls in the SEL skills within the CASEL competency of relationship skills, which include communicating effectively, practicing teamwork and collaborative problem-solving, and resolving conflicts constructively. Discussions of self-awareness and social awareness can look at the conversation that Nana and CJ have, how CJ reacts to the people he sees, and their purpose for the trip, which is revealed in the final pages. The lesson plan at the end of this chapter uses *Last Stop on Market Street* and *Nana in the City* and provides individual and group activities, as well as discussion questions and additional resources.

History

The category of history includes the NCSS strand of time, continuity, and change and the C3 dimension of history. This topic looks at the stories of individuals and groups who have shaped historical change and examines such topics as the chronological sequence of multiple events, comparisons of perspectives of people in the past and present and different accounts of the same event, and discussions of possible reasons for past events or developments and their consequences for the present and future.

Biographies of historically important and famous people provide gripping and inspirational stories that are familiar to many people, but biographies of lesser-known figures, such as *Pies from Nowhere: How Georgia Gilmore Sustained the Montgomery Bus Boycott* by Dee Romit, demonstrate the vital roles of people who did not gain the widespread publicity and fame but demonstrated ingenuity, bravery, creativity, and perseverance in the face of great obstacles. Stories of seemingly small feats of bravery or courage and their impact can highlight to young students how meaningful even the smallest actions can be, highlighting such SEL domains as values, identity, social awareness, and responsible decision-making.

Two specific themes within history provide rich opportunities for discussions of the subject content in conjunction with the SEL themes: stories of immigration and stories of segregation. Through these stories students learn about the events that brought people to America and then separated them within it; they learn about identities, beliefs, and actions of kindness and exclusion.

Stories of immigration. The first theme reflects on the experiences of immigration, with picture books focusing both on the experiences of people coming to America and on the struggles of new immigrants within the country. The story of immigration is an effective lens for examining the C3 strands in history that call on students to examine the same events from different perspectives. It is also helpful in the NCSS theme of time, continuity, and change, to consider questions such as, "How were the ideas and attitudes of people in the past similar to and different from life today?"

All The Way to America: The Story of a Big Italian Family and a Little Shovel by Dan Yaccarino is a funny and loving reflection on the author's family's journey to America and several generations' lives as Italian-American farmers, gardeners, and chefs in New York. The families pass down a small shovel from generation to generation that is used to harvest and measure food in various contexts. *The Memory Coat* by Elvira Woodruff is a more somber story of an immigrant family fleeing anti-Semitic persecution in Russian. As they approach the immigration inspection at Ellis Island they grow increasingly anxious that a boy will be turned back because of his torn and dirty clothes and health problems. Turning a beloved coat inside-out gives the boy the appearance of health and well-being that allows him to pass inspection. *Anita and the Dragons* by Hannah Carmona is the story of a girl in the Dominican Republic who is preparing to immigrate to the United States with her parents and brother, likening the planes she sees pass overhead and the plane she boards to America to dragons. Beautifully illustrated and poignantly written, the text and images portray Anita's sadness at leaving her homeland and extended family and her fears of facing the unknown of a new country: "With one step, I move away from the familiar. With another step, I walk into the unknown. Hand in hand, we stand strong. Bravely, through the dark, narrow throat of the beast, we enter its belly where we will take flight to new adventures."

Picture books that look at the experience of immigrants once they arrive in the United States also provide a variety of viewpoints about the experience of settling in a new land, while offering important lessons on SEL themes such as perspective, identity, and social awareness. *Dreamers* is an autobiographical story by the Mexican-American author Yuri Morales, who describes the unfamiliarity and newness of her life as an immigrant to California with an infant son. She beautifully describes and illustrates the transformative experience of discovering the public library: "Books became our language. Books became our home. Books became our lives. We learned to read, to speak, to write, and to make our voices heard."

My Two Blankets by Irena Kobald and *My Name is Sangoel* by Karen Lynn Williams and Khadra Mohammed tell the stories of immigrant children adjusting to life in the United States, meeting friends and learning the language and culture of their new homes. In *My Two Blankets*, a girl flees war in her homeland to come to the United States but feels alone in an utterly foreign land: "We came to this country to be safe. Everything was strange. The people were strange. The food was strange. The animals and plants were strange. Even the wind felt strange."

She is befriended by a girl in a park, and the friendship becomes a "new blanket" that comforts her as much as memories of her native land. *My Name is Sangoel* is a powerful lesson in treasuring an identity from a homeland, which in Sangoel's case is his name, which is given to generations of men in the Sudanese tribe of the Dinka. When the students and other members of his new community struggle with pronouncing his name, Sangoel comes up with an ingenious phonetic spelling that helps the whole class learn to pronounce each other's names.

These books highlight SEL themes both in the experiences of the immigrants and in the actions of the Americans they meet. They illustrate powerful themes of identity and self-awareness in showing how the immigrants found the courage to leave their home and family and foster such skills as flexibility and resilience to face the challenges of the new land. The books also stress the importance of kindness in showing how the students accept and welcome the new immigrants. These meet the NCSS and C3 standards of comparing multiple perspectives of the same event by showing how immigrants' experiences are both shared and wholly unique.

Themes of segregation. A second theme in this category is the segregation of various groups of people within the United States. There are many excellent picture books on the Civil Rights movement and the segregation of African Americans in the United States, including *Freedom on the Menu* by Carole Boston Weatherford, which is a fictionalized account of the sit-ins in 1960 at a Woolworth's lunch counter in Greensboro, North Carolina. *Freedom Summer* by Deborah Wiles, which won the 2002 Ezra Jack Keats Award and the Coretta Scott King Award, tells the story of a pair of friends—one African American and one white—in Mississippi during the summer of 1964, who find their usual summer activities shut down in acts of defiance by local officials who reject the desegregation legislation of the Civil Rights Act. With children as narrators and protagonists, the books present the realities of segregation in ways that can be felt and understood by children.

Other books on the theme of segregation within different communities include *Separate is Never Equal* by Duncan Tonatiuh, which tells the story of the segregation of Mexican-American students in California schools in the 1940s, and *Write to Me: Letters from Japanese American Children to the Librarian They Left Behind* by Cynthia Grady, a true story of the letters and packages that a librarian in San Diego exchanged with Japanese-American children who were imprisoned during World War II in internment camps. *The Bracelet* by Yoshiko Uchido is a fictional story of a girl sent to the camps, treasuring a bracelet given to her by a friend before her family was forced to leave their home.

The presentation of various points of view of segregation fits in with the C3 Framework that calls on students to examine multiple perspectives regarding the same historical event. Although the time periods of the experiences of the three sets of books differed, the underlying experiences of segregation provide a powerful example to compare and contrast. Several lesson ideas integrate the topic content with SEL domains. Lessons for the theme of immigration can have students reflect on their own families' backgrounds and origins, building around the idea of a community. What makes up a community—is it a shared language? homeland? culture? In the lesson the students can discuss communities that they are part of, from their own family to their neighborhood, religious setting, cultural group, or even a school or club setting. A second way to approach this topic is to have the students reflect on how it felt to come to a new and unfamiliar school, classroom, club, or neighborhood. What emotions were they feeling, and how did those feelings make them act? How did they make new friends? What activities were new or unfamiliar to them? What social and emotional skills did the students use to adapt to their new surroundings and find new friends? All people, including the educators themselves, can recall the feeling of being a new person in an unfamiliar setting, and the sense of uncertainty and fears that come in that setting. Having the children reflect on how they felt, and then think about similar emotions that were shared by children in the books, can help them recognize those emotions in others and respond with support and empathy.

The second theme, of segregation, can be the basis of a powerful lesson around unjust and unfair rules and policies. The civics topic within the C3 Framework contains several standards related to rules, such as "Explain the need for and purposes of rules in various settings inside and outside of school" (D2.Civ.4.K-2). The purpose of rules is a relatively straightforward discussion, especially for older students in the K-3 grade range. But when the lesson looks at how rules can be imposed in a way that limits or punishes one group of people unfairly, the conversation becomes more complicated. Some students will have seen or experienced unequal treatment based on race, appearance, or socio-economic status. Within a setting that feels safe and appropriate for the students, the idea of unfair rules and policies can be explored. A discussion about imposing different rules based on arbitrary characteristics, such as the students' birth month or the color of their shoes, can get across the sense of unfairness. This lesson touches on CASEL domains such as social awareness—identifying diverse social norms, including unjust ones; self-awareness—examining prejudices and biases; and relationship skills, including standing up for the rights of others.

Economics

The topic of economics includes the NCSS strand of production, distribution, and consumption and the C3 strand of economics. It looks at such themes as the benefits and costs of personal decisions, motivations for why people in one country trade goods and services with people in other countries, descriptions of the skills and knowledge required to produce certain goods and services, explanations for how scarcity necessitates decision-making, and the characteristics and use of money. Books on this topic include non-fiction accounts, biographies, and stories that incorporate economic concepts, such as supply and demand, trade, and production of goods. These themes tie in well with SEL domains including good decision-making, problem-solving, and social awareness—recognizing situational demands and opportunities.

Biographies that cover the stands and topics within economics include such books as *No Small Potatoes: Junius G. Groves and His Kingdom in Kansas* by Tonya Bolden, which tells the story of Junius Groves, who was born a slave in the late 1850s or early 1860s in Kentucky. Freed soon after his birth, he travelled to Kansas at the age of 20, where he got a job on a potato farm. After working his way up on the farm, he saved enough to rent and then buy land, eventually growing enough potatoes—approximately 12 million in one year—to earn the title of "Potato King." *No Small Potatoes* describes the steps Junius made in his journey, including the jobs he did and the opportunities and jobs he created for others through his own farm. The story meets the NCSS strand of production, distribution, and consumption, addressing such questions as, "How are goods made, delivered, and used?" It also meets several standards within the C3 Economics strand, including "Describe the skills and knowledge required to produce certain goods and services" (D2.Eco.3.K-2), "Explain how people earn income" (D2.Eco.6.K-2), "Describe examples of capital goods and human capital" (D2.Eco.13.K-2), and "Explain the relationship between investment in human capital, productivity, and future incomes" (D2.Eco.6.3–5). In addition to social studies themes, this book offers excellent cross-curricular opportunities for lessons in science.

The SEL themes met by *No Small Potatoes* include many cognitive and executive functioning themes that look at the plans and decisions that Junius made, as well as SEL themes around perspectives, such as showing grit and perseverance, and self-management, such as setting personal and collective goals, using planning and organizational skills, showing the courage to take initiative and demonstrating personal and collective agency.

Themes of trading and production. A second topic of picture books within the category of economics are those that tell the story of trading goods and services. *A New Coat for Anna* by Harriet Ziefert and the Caldecott Medal-winning picture book *Ox-cart Man* by Donald Hall tell similar stories of barters and trades for goods. Anna needs a new winter coat after the war, when supplies are short and there is little food or money, so her mother trades a watch for wool, a lamp for yarn, and a necklace for weaving. The ox-cart man sells all of his goods—wool, a shawl, mittens, candles, linen, brooms, and other homemade materials, as well as crops from his farm and garden—and, finally, his ox at the market. Readers mourn the loss of the ox-cart man's goods and beloved ox; but with the money he gets in return, he purchases an iron kettle, an embroidery needle, a knife, and other goods to start anew: stitching, whittling, cooking, embroidering, and weaving to make goods that he would sell again in the fall.

Stories about scarcity. The topic of scarcity is beautifully handled in a number of picture books, including *Boxes for Katje* by Candace Fleming and *Maddi's Fridge* by Lois Brandt, which approach the theme from quite different viewpoints. *Boxes for Katje*, based on the author's mother's experience, is the story of a Dutch girl after World War II who receives a box from an American girl named Rosie through the Children's Aid Society in the United States. The box contains soap, chocolate, and socks, all of which Katje shares with her family and the postman. An exchange of letters and increasingly larger deliveries from America continue, culminating in a huge delivery of food, clothing, and soap that is shared throughout Katje's community, who gratefully sends Rosie back a box of Dutch tulips as thanks. *Maddi's Fridge* by Lois Brandt is the story of two friends, Maddi and Sofia, who live in an urban setting portrayed in attractive cartoon illustrations. Sofia learns that Maddi's family does not have enough money for food, but Maddi swears Sofia to secrecy. Sofia brings some food to school for Maddi in ways that go awry—raw fish that get smelly and eggs that break in Sofia's backpack ("Eggs may be good for kids, but eggs are not good for backpacks."). Eventually Sofia tells her mother about Maddi's situation, and they bring over groceries and Maddi forgives Sofia for not keeping her secret.

The two books are lessons in kindness, empathy, and friendship, as well as social awareness and decision-making. A sample lesson related to this book could focus on Junius' story and his life experience. What experiences did Junius have in his childhood that led him to make the decisions he made as he grew up? What SEL traits did he demonstrate as he worked to buy and develop his own farm?

A second lesson related to this theme revolves around setting up a market within the class. Students could take different roles in the market, from producers of the products to consumers and managers, and a multitude of decisions will need to be made, from the products to be sold to how they would be produced and priced. The students would discuss what currency would be used to purchase products and how that currency could be earned. The planning and implementation of the market requires many cognitive SEL skills as well as good decision-making, good communication, and conflict management. Depending on the roles given to the students, other SEL domains such as perspective and self-awareness could be brought into the lesson, as students learn about scarcity and abundance.

Geography

The category of geography includes the NCSS strand of people, places, and environments and looks at such topics as maps; weather and climate; discussions of cultural and environmental characteristics of places and how human activities affect them; questions about how people change the environment and how the environment influences human activity; explanations of why and how people, goods, and ideas move from place to place; and discussions of ways that a catastrophic disaster may affect people living in a place. This wide-ranging category has opportunities for exploring SEL themes that are rooted in a person's place in the world. Topics within the Harvard domain of identity focus on fostering an understanding of one's identity and place in the world and the diversity of identities within communities. The CASEL competency of social awareness includes skills such as taking other students' perspectives, recognizing situational demands and opportunities, and understanding the influences of organizations and systems on behavior. Discussions of responsible decision-making pull in the impact of decisions and beliefs around a person's place in the world: how do the decisions you make about how you define and live in your space affect your community and the world's well-being?

Biographies. Picture books on this topic fit into a similarly wide range of topics. A straightforward category of geography books that beautifully demonstrate SEL themes are biographies of important figures, such as explorers and environmentalists, which is an area that offers excellent cross-curricular opportunities when taught in conjunction with science lessons. One example is *Night Flight: Amelia Earhart Crosses the Atlantic* by Robert Burleigh, which tells the story of Amelia's 1932 solo flight across the Atlantic Ocean, the second solo trans-Atlantic flight and the first by a woman. *Night Flight* describes the fears and physical dangers that Amelia overcame in the face of darkness, fatigue, and treacherous storms as she made her historic flight. It supports C3 Framework standards, including using maps, graphs, photographs and other representations to describe places. Students can track Amelia's flight across the Atlantic using the text description. Using *Night Flight* or another biography in this category, a lesson plan could have the students trace the route or area that the explorer travelled in and narrate the journey or use clay or play dough to create a 3-dimensional map of the route or area that their explorer charted. Individual activities include having the students create a journal entry for their explorer, with at least four entries describing a day in their life with details of what the explorer saw and how they may have reacted or felt. What challenges, dangers, or obstacles did the explorer face, and how did they overcome them? A full-group discussion would circle back to the key questions at the beginning of this chapter: "What impact did the explorer have on the world?" and "What would the world be like today if that person had not existed?" These questions tie into such SEL domains as decision-making, cognitive skills, and social awareness.

Geography stories. A second group of picture books in this category include stories that weave in narratives about geographical and physical features. Narrative picture books such as *River* by Elisha Cooper provide subject content within a fictional story. *River* tells the story of a girl setting out on a journey in a canoe, describing her path, supplies, and the animals and natural surroundings that she sees on the way. Each page spread contains multiple small pictures and text blocks, reiterating the steps of the journey and highlighting the decision-making and other SEL skills that she uses along the way.

The theme in the C3 Frameworks of the interactions of people and the environment is beautifully illustrated and described by pictures books such as *House Held Up By Trees* by Ted Kooser, a solemn reflection on the cycles of nature. In the story, a single father and his two small children live in a house in a rural area. He meticulously tends the land around the house as the children play nearby. As he ages and his children move away, the work becomes too much for him and he, too, leaves the house, which falls into disrepair. Over the years, seedlings sprout around the house and grow into trees, lifting the house into the sky: "The trees lifted it and lifted it, and maybe you will drive past it today or tomorrow, as it floats there above the group like a tree house, a house in the trees, a house held together by the strength of trees, and the wind blowing, perfumed by little green flowers." The book has a sadness that some children might find challenging, but it offers a message of the enduring power of nature.

The Gardener by Sarah Stewart and *The Curious Garden* by Peter Brown share a similar theme of the power of nature, but this time in an urban setting. *The Gardener*, which won the Caldecott Honor, tells the story through letters and cleverly detailed illustrations of a girl sent to a big city to live with her seemingly gruff uncle, a baker, after her father loses his job. She transforms the uncle's rooftop and front sidewalk into a lush garden, bringing joy to her family and the neighborhood. *The Curious Garden* is the story of a boy, Liam, in an urban setting devoid of greenery: "There once was a city without gardens or trees or greenery of any kind. Most people spent their time indoors. As you can imagine, it was a very dreary place." The book's vivid illustrations show Liam emerging onto a rooftop to find a few dying plants. He nurses them back to life and prompts an urban renewal of greenery, with the final spread showing the city with a sunny, green landscape of rooftop gardens and green lawns. Both books offer a powerful lesson of how humans can change an environment, but also how a single person can have a large impact. Planting a single plant is the first step in a journey that transforms the physical landscape as well as the social and emotional perspectives of the neighborhood. Relevant SEL domains include cognitive skills such as task-initiation (starting a garden), problem-solving, and working through challenges; CASEL competencies such as social awareness, responsible decision-making, and social awareness all are highlighted in these stories. A lesson related to this theme could work with setting up a classroom garden or window box, starting with the tasks to build and tend to it and building up to the uses for the plants that are grown in it. A larger lesson could include discussions around a community garden and the efforts required to grow, harvest, and distribute the plants within it and lessons of urban renewal and transformation, from turning abandoned plots of land planting rooftop gardens in large urban settings.

Identity and Culture

The final category within the theme of social studies is identity and culture, which includes the two NCSS strands of culture, individual development and identity, and global connections, and touches on many of the themes in the four topics of the C3 Framework. This topic helps students understand varied perspectives by looking at similarities, differences, beliefs, values, cohesion, and diversity. It addresses such questions as:

- ◆ How does culture unify a group of people?
- ◆ How have others influenced who I am and who I am becoming?
- ◆ How can institutions help to meet individual needs and promote the common good?
- ◆ How do choices I make influence who I am and how others see me?
- ◆ How are people, places, and environments connected around the globe?

The complex idea of identity being rooted in multiple heritages and traditions is presented in two books, *Where Are You From?* by Yamila Mendez and *Eyes That Kiss in the Corners* by Joanna Ho. *Where Are You From?* features a child reflecting on the questions from her friends and classmates about where she is from. "I'm from here, from today, same as everyone else, I say. No, where are you *really* from? they insist." These questions lead her to her *abuelo*, who, like her, "looks like he doesn't belong." He describes the land of her ancestors—"the Pampas, the open, free land . . . the gaucho, brave and strong . . . from the mountains so high they tickle Señor Cielo's belly." He finishes by declaring, "You? You are from all of us."

Eyes That Kiss in the Corners also considers appearance as an indicator of difference and otherness, as a girl compares her eyes, which "kiss in the corners and glow like warm tea," to her friends' eyes, which are "like sapphire lagoons with lashes like lace trim on ballgowns." The girl compares her eyes to her mother's and her grandmother's (Amah) eyes, and to her baby sister's. Like *Where Are You From?* the book looks across generations to take pride in the family's history and cultural heritage.

The question of what it means to be American, and the celebration of diversity, is addressed through brief, eloquent text and bold pictures in *We Came to America* by Faith Ringgold, which is dedicated "to all the children who come to America." Beginning with Native Americans, who "were already here," Ringgold describes the arrivals of all groups—immigrants and slaves—every "color, race, and religion," bringing their stories, music, art, and food. These books celebrate diversity, recognizing that beauty and strength is rooted in the different viewpoints, talents, and gifts that people contribute.

A powerful collection of picture books look at the experiences of Black Americans. *I, Too, Am America* by Langston Hughes, which won the Coretta Scott King Award, and *The Undefeated* by Kwame Alexander, which won the Caldecott Medal and a Newberry Honor, both celebrate the contributions and mourn the injustices experienced by Black Americans. *The Undefeated* is a poem that Alexander wrote in 2008, after the birth of his second daughter; it shows a range of images of African Americans, including Jesse Owens, an enslaved family, and many notable Black artists, athletes, political leaders and Civil Rights heroes. "This is for the unforgettable. The swift and sweet ones who hurdled history and opened a world of possible." *I, Too, Am America* is a poem as well, by Langston Hughes, illustrated by Bryan Collier as a story about Black Pullman porters on a transcontinental railway, vital but almost invisible to most travelers. The image of an American flag is woven through the illustrations, growing more prominent through the book. Collier writes in an illustrator's note that the flag "acts as a metaphor for the growth of our people in this country, almost invisible during the Pullman porter's time—just as he was even though he worked every day in plain sight—but bolder and stronger toward the end, no longer invisible and ignored."

Questions of identity that run through these books are tied closely with the C3 Frameworks for grades 3–5, specifically "Explain why individuals and groups during the same historical period differed in their perspectives" (D2.His.4.3–5) and "Explain connections among historical contexts and people's perspectives at the time" (D2.His.5.3–5). They address NCSS themes within the strands of Individual Development and Identity, such as, "How am I different from and similar to others?" and "How have others influenced who I am and who I am becoming?" These themes offer powerful illustrations of SEL themes including self-awareness, such as integrating personal and social identities and identifying personal, cultural, and linguistic assets. In the domain of social awareness, these lessons touch on the themes of taking others' perspectives and demonstrating empathy and compassion. Within the Harvard domain of identity, the content and picture books help foster students' sense of place in the world and an understanding of the diversity of identities within local and global communities.

The sense of being linked across the world can be taught in lessons that explore the lives and experiences of other children, through organizations that let students correspond with each other, such as PenPal Schools, or interact through video apps with other schools. Mystery Skype allows classes to connect with another class and ask a series of questions that help them guess where each class is located, which also pulls in the geography standards from the C3 Framework. Having students see and interact with other students their age and allowing them to see the similarities and differences between their lives is a powerful lesson in defining identity and culture.

The enormous variety of topics covered within social studies in the lower elementary grades opens up myriad opportunities for discussions of SEL. Rooting lessons in the three key questions (Why did this happen? What were the consequences? What would the world be like without this event or person?) helps students focus on decisions and consequences while widening their perspective and fostering empathy. The picture books in this category offer many openings for showing students the roles and responsibilities that they can take on and the impact that just a single person can make through such seemingly small acts as voting, tending to the environment, or offering acts of kindness to those in need. Understanding aspects of a student's identity that are both unique and shared, and seeing how interconnected we are across the globe, help foster a sense of global responsibility and increases perspectives and empathy.

LESSON PLAN

Title and Grade:
My Community Grade: K or 1
Standards and Learning Objectives
C3 Framework: • Geography, D2.Geo.3.K-2: "Use maps, globes, and other simple geographic models to identify cultural and environmental characteristics of places" **NCSS:** • Culture: Theme questions for exploration, "How are groups of people alike and different?" and "What is cultural diversity, and how does diversity develop both within and across cultures?"

English Language Arts Common Core:
- **Reading: Literature**
  - RL.1.2. Retell stories, including key details, and demonstrate understanding of their central message or lesson.
  - RL.1.3. Describe characters, settings, and major events in a story, using key details.
- **Speaking and Listening:**
  - SL.1.2. Ask and answer questions about key details in a text read aloud or information presented orally or through other media.
  - SL.1.4. Describe people, places, things, and events with relevant details, expressing ideas and feelings clearly.

SEL Standards: CASEL
- Social awareness: Taking others' perspectives, identifying diverse social norms
- Relationship skills: Communicating effectively, practicing teamwork and collaborative problem-solving, and resolving conflicts constructively

SEL Standards: Harvard
- Identity: Developing a sense of identity and place in the world, and fostering an understanding of the diversity of identities within local and global communities

Learning Objectives

After reading two texts with the focus on the concept of community, the students will identify key features of a community, discuss similarities and differences of communities, and describe how communities shape the lives of their members, through individual and small-group final projects.

ASSESSMENT

Informal assessment will include assessment of students' participation in whole- and small-group discussions and completion of the daily activities. Assessments will vary

based on the level of the students; a suggested differentiated assessment would be:
- **Level 1:** Students will be able to discuss key details from the text, including characters and plot details. They will be able to describe their own community and discuss the features and members of it.
- **Level 2:** Students will be able to summarize the plot and use textual and graphic clues to describe the characters' emotions. They will be able to discuss how people contribute to a community—who are the community helpers? How do people work with and help each other in a community? What does it mean to belong to a community—what emotions and responsibilities come with that?
- **Level 3:** Students will be able to summarize the plot and characters and discuss how aspects of the community and neighborhoods are presented in the text, using specific examples. They will be able to compare and contrast different communities and discuss the idea of diversity within and between communities.

LEARNING PLAN

Instructional Resources and Materials

- *Last Stop on Market Street* by Matt de la Peña
- *Nana in the City* by Lauren Castillo
- Butcher paper or large sheets of paper for drawing a community/neighborhood
- Markers, pens, and pencils (if drawing the maps) OR clay or play dough
- Sample of a neighborhood map that shows the components that students could include on their own

Daily Plans

Stage 1: Group Activity (1 Day)
Watch this clip: Sesame Street: "My Home" www.youtube.com/watch?v=noxDzH9PE-4
Do a read-aloud of one of the following books:
- *Thank you, Omu!* by Oge Mora
- *Hey, Wall! A Story of Art and Community* by Susan Verde

Discuss the concept of community:
- What is a community?
- What sorts of people and places would you find in a rural community? An urban community? A suburban community?
- Who are the people in your community?
- How are they similar to and different from you?
- How do people in a community work together to help each other?

Stage 2: Read Aloud and Activities (2 Days)
Read aloud *Last Stop on Market Street* by Matt de la Peña and *Nana in the City* by Lauren Castillo. Using the CROWD strategy described in Chapter 4, or another format to guide your development of discussion questions, ask students a variety of questions that allow them to develop their understanding of the key points in the text, including those that are directly stated and those that must be inferred. One model might be "Thick" and "Thin" questions, with thick questions that require some thinking or finding evidence from the text and thin questions that are straightforward. Examples include:
- **Thin:** Where were CJ and Nana going on the bus?
- **Thick:** How did the author and illustrator of *Last Stop on Market Street* show diversity in the community?
- **Thin:** Why was the boy afraid of the city?
- **Thick:** What made the boy change his mind about the city?

On the second day of this stage, small groups of students will re-read the books. If needed, students can work with the teacher or teaching assistant, or listen to an audio version of the story. They can either be given a piece of paper to document their thinking, or they can discuss and share their discussion with the whole class. Questions could include:
- Where were CJ and Nana going?
- Why was CJ unhappy on the trip?

- How did Nana interact with the people on their journey?
- How did CJ compare himself with the people on his journey?
- What did CJ learn on his journey?
- Why was Clara unhappy in the city?
- Why did Clara change her mind about the city by the end of the book?

Stage 3: Differentiated Learning (3–4 Days—1½ Days per Project)
Learners' individual needs will be met through differentiation of content, process, and product. Activities can be individually focused or completed in small groups.

Individual activities : Have the students choose two activities, at least one of which challenges them. Each student will explain his or her choices. Make sure all students will need the same amount of time to complete their activities.

Level 1:
1. Students should put the story pieces in order and match vocabulary to meanings.
2. Students should draw and describe the neighborhood in which they live.
3. Students should speak on video/audio* about the emotions/feelings in the text and their own responses to it.

Level 2:
1. Students should draw and describe the neighborhood they live in, describing the components.
2. Students should describe on video/audio* how CJ's and/or the boy's feelings about the community changed throughout the books.
3. Students should compare the people and sights that CJ and Nana's grandson saw during their time in the city, including buildings, natural landmarks, and people.

Level 3:
1. Using supervision and support as needed, students will create a presentation about how people make up a community and what it means to be part of a community. Who are community helpers? How do people within a community help each other and their neighborhood?
2. On a large piece of paper or posterboard, draw a grid. On squares or rectangles, students will draw out components of a city, including houses, parks, schools, apartment buildings, skyscrapers, roads, and hospitals, and lay them out on the grid to design a city. They should include natural features such as rivers, lakes, and forests.*

*Adapted from *Cities: Discover How they Work* by Kathleen Reilly (Nomad Press, 2014).

Group project:
In small groups, students will create a community of their own. What will it be named? What kind of community will it be (rural, suburban, urban)? What type of people live in it? Who are the community helpers? What are the main community buildings and features of the community?

Stage 4: Revisit Group Activity (1 Day)
On the first day, students were introduced to the concept of a community. On this final day, students can reflect on two aspects of the lesson: the physical components of a community and the human aspect of belonging to a community.
- Physical components of a community: The two books were centered on urban communities; what differences and similarities were there in terms of the physical components? What differences and similarities would there be between those communities and a rural community? What features do rural and urban communities have in common?
- Membership in a community: CJ was uncomfortable about some of the differences in the people he saw on his trip. How are communities diverse? How do people work together in a community, despite their differences, to help and support each other? What examples could you find of that in the books?

> **References**
>
> Castillo, L. (2014). *Nana in the city*. Clarion Books.
> de la Peña, Matt. (2015). *Last stop on Market Street* (C. Robinson, Illus.). G.P. Putnam's Sons Books for Young Readers.
> Mora, O. (2018). *Thank you, Omu!* Little, Brown.
> Reilly, K. (2014). *Cities: Discover how they work* (T. Casteel, Illus.). Nomad Press.
> Verde, S. (2018). *Hey, wall! A story of art and community* (J. Parra, Illus.). Simon & Schuster.

References

Aslan, D., & Köksal Akyol, A. (2020). Impact of an empathy training program on children's perspective-taking abilities. *Psychological Reports*, *123*(6), 2394–2409.

Eisenberg, N., Eggum, N. D., & Di Giunta, L. (2010). Empathy-related responding: Associations with prosocial behavior, aggression, and intergroup relations. *Social Issues and Policy Review*, *4*(1), 143.

Feshbach, N., & Feshbach, S. (2009). Empathy and education. In J. Decety & W. Ickes (Eds), *The social neuroscience of empathy* (pp. 85–98). MIT Press.

National Council for the Social Studies. (2013). *The college, career, and civic life (C3) framework for social studies state standards: Guidance for enhancing the rigor of k-12 civics, economics, geography, and history*. National Council for the Social Studies (NCSS). Washington, DC.

National curriculum standards for social studies: A framework for teaching, learning, and assessment. (2010). National Council for the Social Studies (NCSS). Washington, DC.

Ornaghi, V., Conte, E., & Grazzani, I. (2020). Empathy in toddlers: The role of emotion regulation, language ability, and maternal emotion socialization style. *Frontiers in Psychology*, *11*, 2844.

Spinrad, T. L., & Gal, D. E. (2018). Fostering prosocial behavior and empathy in young children. *Current Opinion in Psychology*, *20*, 40–44. https://doi.org/10.1016/j.copsyc.2017.08.004

Walsh, E., & Walsh, D. (2019, May 9). How children develop empathy. *Psychology Today*. www.psychologytoday.com/us/blog/smart-parenting-smarter-kids/201905/how-children-develop-empathy

Book List

Civics, Community, and Government

Castillo, L. (2014). *Nana in the city*. Clarion Books.
de la Peña, Matt. (2015). *Last stop on Market Street* (C. Robinson, Illus.). G.P. Putnam's Sons Books for Young Readers.
Diesen, D. (2020). *Equality's call: The story of voting rights in America* (M. Mora, Illus.). Beach Lane Books.
Eggers, D. (2018). *What can a citizen do?* (S. Harris, Illus.). Chronicle Books.
McNamara, M. (2020). *Vote for our future!* (M. Player, Illus.). Schwartz & Wade.
Mora, O. (2018). *Thank you, Omu!* Little, Brown.
Verde, S. (2018). *Hey, wall: A story of art and community* (J. Parra, Illus.). Simon & Schuster/Paula Wiseman Books.
Verde, S. (2020). *Oye, Muro* (A. Romay, Trans.; J. Parra, Illus.). Simon & Schuster/Paula Wiseman Books.

History

Carmona, H. (2021). *Anita and the dragons* (A. Cunha, Illus.). Lantana Publishing.
Grady, C. (2019). *Write to me: Letters from Japanese American children to the librarian they left behind* (A. Hirao, Illus.). Charlesbridge.
Kobald, I. (2015). *My two blankets* (F. Blackwood, Illus.). HMH Books for Young Readers.
Markel, M. (2013). *Brave girl: Clara and the shirtwaist makers' strike of 1909* (M. Sweet, Illus.). Balzer + Bray.
Morales, Y. (2018). *Dreamers*. Neal Porter Books.
Morales, Y. (2018). *Soñadores*. Neal Porter Books.
Pickney, A. D. (2010). *Sit-in: How four friends stood up by sitting down* (B. Pinkney, Illus.). Little, Brown and Company.
Romit, D. (2018). *Pies from nowhere: How Georgia Gilmore sustained the Montgomery bus boycott* (L. Freeman, Illus.). little bee books.
Tonatiuh, D. (2014). *Separate is never equal: Sylvia Mendez & her family's fight for desegregation* (D. Tonatiuh, Illus.). Abrams Books for Young Readers.
Uchida, Y. (1996). *The bracelet* (J. Yardley, Illus.). Puffin Books.
Weatherford, C. B. (2007). *Freedom on the menu: The Greensboro sit-ins* (J. Lagarrigue, Illus.). Puffin Books.

Wiles, D. (2005). *Freedom summer* (J. Lagarrigue, Illus.). Aladdin.
Williams, K. L. & Mohammed, K. (2009). *My name is Sangoel* (C. Stock, Illus.). Eerdmans Books for Young Readers.
Woodruff, E. (1999). *The memory coat* (M. Dooling, Illus.). Scholastic Press.
Yaccarino, D. (2014). *All the way to America: The story of a big Italian family and a little shovel*. Dragonfly Books.

Economics
Bolden, T. (2018). *No small potatoes: Junius G. Groves and his kingdom in Kansas* (D. Tate, Illus.). Knopf Books for Young Readers.
Brandt, L. (2014). *Maddi's fridge* (V. Vogel, Illus.). Flashlight Press.
Fleming, C. (2003). *Boxes for Katje* (S. Dressen-McQueen, Illus.). Farrar, Straus and Giroux.
Hall, D. (1983). *Ox-cart man* (B. Cooney, Illus.). Puffin Books.
Ziefert, H. (1988). *A new coat for Anna* (A. Lobel, Illus.). Dragonfly Books.

Geography
Brown, P. (2009). *The curious garden*. Little, Brown Books for Young Readers.
Burleigh, R. (2011). *Night flight: Amelia Earhart crosses the Atlantic* (W. Minor, Illus.). Simon & Schuster/Paula Wiseman Books.
Cooper, E. (2019). *River*. Orchard Books.
Kooser, T. (2012). *House held up by trees* (J. Klassen, Illus.). Candlewick.
Stewart, S. (2007). *The gardener* (D. Small, Illus.). Square Fish.

Identity and Culture
Alexander, K. (2019). *The undefeated* (K. Nelson, Illus.). Versify.
Danticat, E. (2015). *Mama's nightingale: A story of immigration and separation* (L. Staub, Illus.) Dial Books.
Díaz, J. (2018). *Islandborn* (L. Espinosa, Illus.). Dial Books.
Ho, J. (2021). *Eyes that kiss in the corners* (D. Ho, Illus.). HarperCollins.
Hughes, L. (2012). *I, too, am America* (B. Collier, Illus.). Simon & Schuster Books for Young Readers.
Lindstrom, C. (2020). *We are water protectors* (M. Goade, Illus.). Roaring Brook Press.
Méndez, Y. S. (2019a). *¿De dónde eres?: Where are you from?* (J. Kim, Illus.). HarperCollins Espanol.
Méndez, Y. S. (2019b). *Where are you from?* (J. Kim, Illus.). HarperCollins.

Phi, B. (2017). *A different pond* (T. Bui, Illus.). Capstone Young Readers.

Ringgold, F. (2016). *We came to America*. Knopf Books for Young Readers.

Stewart, S. (2012). *The quiet place* (D. Small, Illus.). Farrar, Straus and Giroux.

7

Integrating SEL and ELA Using Literary Texts

Literary picture books provide innumerable opportunities to link social and emotional learning (SEL) with learning in the English language arts (ELA). Inherent in the structure of most stories is a character who is experiencing some sort of conflict, and through managing that conflict, the character experiences a range of emotions and experiences. When children are young, they learn about literary elements (e.g., characters, setting, plot, conflict, and theme). Perhaps teachers even ask them to write a story summary using the frame: "Somebody, wanted, but, so, then" (e.g., The three little pigs wanted to stay safe from the wolf, but some of their homes weren't well made and collapsed. So, they hid in the brick house. Then the wolf couldn't eat them.) As children move into upper elementary grades and beyond, they are introduced formally to different types of conflict (e.g., person vs. self, person vs. person, person vs. society). Even in the early elementary grades, it is in this conflict that powerful SEL lessons begin. How did the character/individual understand and manage an internal conflict? That is self-awareness and self-management. How did the character/person resolve a conflict with another person? That question leads directly to relationship skills. Is there a broader conflict with community that can be considered? This is social awareness. Additionally, each of these types of conflict can lead to fruitful conversations about responsible decision-making as students consider whether the choices made were constructive or not.

Additionally, the Common Core State Standards (CCSS), while providing a framework for ELA instruction, leave plenty of room for the integration of SEL within the teaching of the standards. The introductory material to the CCSS notes that students who meet the standards "actively seek the wide, deep, and thoughtful engagement with high-quality literary and informational texts that builds knowledge, enlarges experience, and broadens worldviews" (National Governors Association Center for Best Practices & Council of Chief State School Officers, 2010, p. 3). It is in this "thoughtful engagement" with texts that expand the depth and breadth of students' experiences and understanding of the world that connections between SEL and development of proficiency in ELA can be found. The CCSS document supports and encourages these connections when it notes that educators should include an emphasis on "such matters as social, emotional, and physical development and approaches to learning" (p. 6). Thankfully, thoughtfully chosen, well-written picture books provide a perfect foundation for integrating the teaching of SEL skills with ELA standards.

Integration With the English Language Arts

A look at the Common Core College and Career Readiness (CCR) anchor standards, which provide a broad overview of what students should learn in ELA, illustrates many opportunities for connections between ELA and SEL. These standards are organized into four main categories: reading, writing, speaking and listening, and language, and each category has specific standards for each grade level. The broad category of reading includes the subcategories of literature, informational text, and foundational skills. From this list of key skills, thinking about ways to integrate SEL with ELA provides educators with an abundance of riches. Simply put, just about any text chosen to teach an SEL-related theme could be used to teach an ELA standard, and with any ELA standard a teacher could find a relevant picture book that addresses an SEL competency.

An example can help illustrate this point. Kindergarten teachers may start the school year by teaching or reviewing basic concepts of print, such as the fact that words go from left to right, top to bottom. This is a set of skills that could be addressed with any text, but a teacher who wants to begin to integrate SEL into daily teaching could choose to read aloud a book like *The Day You Begin* by Jacqueline Woodson. This book helps anxious students identify their own concerns about not fitting in, while at the same time acknowledging the importance of being oneself. This same teacher might ask students to share with a peer their own experiences of feeling different, thus supporting the first CCSS anchor standard for speaking and listening, which asks that students "prepare for and participate effectively in a range of conversations and collaborations with diverse partners, building on others' ideas and expressing their own clearly and persuasively about particular text" (NGACBP & CCSS, 2010, p. 22). With this initial lesson, perhaps on one of the first days of school, a teacher has addressed several ELA standards as well as the Collaborative for Academic, Social, and Emotional Learning (CASEL) competencies of self-awareness, self-management, social awareness, and relationship skills. With assistance, children in this kindergarten classroom have begun to identify their own similarities and differences, celebrate the differences in others, share their opinions, and listen to others.

Approaching planning from a different perspective, teachers might begin with a particular SEL standard or text that relates to a challenge the students are having in the classroom. A teacher could choose a text like *The Many Colors of Harpreet Singh* by Supriya Kelkar, which addresses a Sikh boy's wearing of a turban, or *Hair Love* by Matthew A. Cherry, which celebrates a black girl's curls and her dad who helps her style them just right, for multiple purposes. These books address broader SEL themes of difference, belonging, and family, provide an opportunity for diverse students to see themselves represented in texts, and allow students from majority cultures to learn more about the experiences of their classmates who are different from them. At the same time, these books, like many others, provide numerous opportunities for students to address the broad range of ELA standards as they consider characters and plot, support their thinking with evidence from the text, and talk and write about what they have read.

Within this context, Chapters 7 and 8 focus on lessons with authentic texts that serve as a basis for the integration of SEL and ELA. We assume that teachers are also identifying their students' needs in such foundational areas as phonics, word study, fluency, and even handwriting. These chapters do not address these important ELA topics, but we trust that the readers are including them, as needed, in their comprehensive literacy programs. As noted earlier, these can be supported and developed using texts that support SEL skills, but many teachers may find that there is a need for explicit instruction in these foundational concepts, just as they may use a specific SEL curriculum to support students' development. Our goal in the next two chapters, which focus on the use of literary and informational texts, is to wade through the innumerable possibilities for SEL-ELA integration and suggest some that are the most powerful and meaningful, within the context of a broader literacy program.

Table 7.1 provides initial suggestions for making connections between CCSS anchor standards, specific grade level standards for literary texts, and the competencies and domains from CASEL and Harvard. These are clearly only a few of the possible areas of integration, and as you read, we imagine you will be thinking about the books that you use with your students and considering options for integration with your specific ELA standards and SEL skills.

Table 7.1 Sample Common Core State Standards and Related SEL Competencies

Sample CCSS Anchor Standard	Specific Grade-Level Standards	SEL Competencies and Domains
Reading Standard 2 Determine central ideas or themes of a text and analyze their development; summarize the key supporting details and ideas	Literary Texts • *Kindergarten*: With prompting and support, retell familiar stories, including key details. • *First Grade*: Retell stories, including key details, and demonstrate understanding of their central message or lesson. • *Second Grade*: Recount stories, including fables and folktales from diverse cultures, and determine their central message, lesson, or moral. • *Third Grade*: Recount stories, including fables, folktales, and myths from diverse cultures; determine the central message, lesson, or moral and explain how it is conveyed through key details in the text.	Self-awareness Emotion Values Perspectives Identity

(*Continued*)

Table 7.1 (Continued)

Sample CCSS Anchor Standard	Specific Grade-Level Standards	SEL Competencies and Domains
Reading Standard 3 Analyze how and why individuals, events, and ideas develop and interact over the course of a text.	*Literary Texts* • *Kindergarten*: With prompting and support, identify characters, settings, and major events in a story. • *First grade*: With prompting and support, identify characters, settings, and major events in a story • *Second grade*: Describe characters, settings, and major events in a story, using key details • *Third grade*: Describe characters in a story (e.g., their traits, motivations, or feelings) and explain how their actions contribute to the sequence of events.	Responsible decision-making Cognitive Social Values Perspectives
Reading Standard 6 Assess how point of view or purpose shapes the content and style of a text.	*Literary Texts* • *Kindergarten*: With prompting and support, name the author and illustrator of a story and define the role of each in telling the story. • *First Grade*: Identify who is telling the story at various points in a text. • *Second grade*: Acknowledge differences in the points of view of characters, including by speaking in a different voice for each character when reading dialogue aloud. • *Third grade*: Distinguish their own point of view from that of the narrator or those of the characters.	Social awareness Social Values Perspectives
Writing Standard 1 Write arguments to support claims in an analysis of substantive topics or texts, using valid reasoning and relevant and sufficient evidence.	• *Kindergarten*: Use a combination of drawing, dictating, and writing to compose opinion pieces in which children tell a reader the topic or the name of the book they are writing about and state an opinion or preference about the topic or book (e.g., My favorite book is . . .). • *First grade*: Write opinion pieces in which they introduce the topic or name the book they are writing about, state an opinion, supply a reason for the opinion, and provide some sense of closure. • *Second grade*: Write opinion pieces in which they introduce the topic or book they are writing about, state an opinion, supply reasons that support the opinion, use linking words (e.g., because, and, also) to connect opinion and reasons, and provide a concluding statement or section.	Relationship skills Social Perspectives Identity

Sample CCSS Anchor Standard	Specific Grade-Level Standards	SEL Competencies and Domains
	• *Third grade*: Write opinion pieces on topics or texts, supporting a point of view with reasons. a. Introduce the topic or text they are writing about, state an opinion, and create an organizational structure that lists reasons. b. Provide reasons that support the opinion. c. Use linking words and phrases (e.g., *because, therefore, since, for example*) to connect opinion and reasons. d. Provide a concluding statement or section.	
Writing Standard 3 Write narratives to develop real or imagined experiences or events using effective technique, well-chosen details, and well-structured event sequences.	• *Kindergarten*: Use a combination of drawing, dictating, and writing to narrate a single event or several loosely linked events, tell about the events in the order in which they occurred, and provide a reaction to what happened. • *First grade*: Write narratives in which they recount two or more appropriately sequenced events, include some details regarding what happened, use temporal words to signal event order, and provide some sense of closure. • *Second grade*: Write narratives in which they recount a well-elaborated event or short sequence of events; include details to describe actions, thoughts, and feelings; use temporal words to signal event order; and provide a sense of closure. • *Third grade*: Write narratives to develop real or imagined experiences or events using effective technique, descriptive details, and clear event sequences. a. Establish a situation and introduce a narrator and/or characters; organize an event sequence that unfolds naturally. b. Use dialogue and descriptions of actions, thoughts, and feelings to develop experiences and events or show the response of characters to situations. c. Use temporal words and phrases to signal event order. d. Provide a sense of closure.	Self-management Emotion Cognitive

The following section focuses on the narrative literary texts that can serve as exemplars for integrating SEL with the ELA CCSS. Within the category of literary text in this chapter, we have focused on stories, although dramas and poetry also fall within this category. We found that stories, with their clearly defined literary elements, including characters and plot, led to more options for integration, although there is clearly space for adding texts outside of stories to your list for ELA-SEL integration.

Literary Text Exemplars

The complex literary texts described in this section were chosen because they serve the literacy and SEL needs of the diverse children in early elementary classrooms. Hoffman, Teale, and Yokota (2015) remind readers that quality children's literature "can support read-aloud experiences through which teachers apprentice children into complex processing of texts" (p. 11). While their article focused primarily on using read-alouds to support students' work with complex texts, their point holds true for whatever types of reading experiences work best for a group of students. For many younger, or less proficient, readers these texts will be a meaningful way for a teacher to integrate SEL competencies and ELA standards by reading aloud. For older, or more proficient readers, these same texts can be read independently or in small groups with some support from the teacher.

In this chapter and the next, for each CASEL SEL competency, one picture book is highlighted to demonstrate the integration with an ELA anchor standard. Connections to the broader Harvard SEL domains are also noted. In addition to the one exemplar text, following each category, two additional texts addressing the same CASEL competency at differing levels of complexity are included. These texts will assist teachers in meeting the needs of all students in the K-3 grade band. In a classroom where, for example, a grade-level text is used for read-aloud, the other texts can be used by individuals or small groups at differing reading levels to continue the consideration of the SEL competency.

Self-Awareness

The Name Jar by Yangsook Choi and *My Name is Sangoel* by Karen Lynn Williams and Khadra Mohammed (referenced in Chapter 6) address similar themes of identity and acceptance by considering a universal topic: one's name and where it came from. *Sangoel* is a family name, one that represents the Dinka tribe in Northern Sudan. In *The Name Jar*, Unhei, the main character, has an ethnic name that represents her Korean heritage. While her friends offered to help her pick an American name, and even created a name jar filled with different options, in the end Unhei tells her class:

> "I realized that I liked my name best, so I chose it again. Korean names mean something. Unhei means *grace*."

These two books provide a wonderful opportunity for students to develop their self-awareness skills in an age-appropriate way. Broadly, many children may experience some disconnect between the identities they have in their home and communities, and the identities that are seen as the "norm" in schools. These books acknowledge this disconnect and suggest ways that children can manage them, while at the same time promoting the idea that it is OK to be different. For students whose names and identities are more "typical," these texts provide opportunities to discuss the feelings of others, identify the ways students can be welcoming, and consider what biases they may have regarding those aspects of a person's identity that might be different from their own.

The CASEL competency of self-awareness, and the emotion, values, perspectives, and identity Harvard domains, also provide a meaningful opportunity to connect with the CCR reading anchor standard 2: "Determine central ideas or themes of a text and analyze their development; summarize the key supporting details and ideas." The youngest children can retell the story, perhaps explaining what happened at the beginning, middle, and end, but as children get older, more sophisticated in their thinking, or with guidance and support from the teacher, they will be able to understand the message or moral. Additionally, when two books are available with similar themes as with

My Name is Sangoel and *The Name Jar*, teachers are able to provide a model for how to infer key ideas. In the classroom, a teacher could model how to use text evidence to identify a theme using one of the texts, and then allow individuals or small groups to read the second text and complete the same process.

> **Self-Awareness Book Suggestions**
>
> *Julián is a Mermaid* by Jessica Love (190L)
> *I am Henry Finch* by Alexis Deacon (AD460L)
> *The Name Jar* by Yangsook Choi (AD 590L)

Self-Management

After the Fall: How Humpty Dumpty Got Back Up Again by Dan Santat expresses, through characters and language appropriate for young children, the difficulties inherent in trying to get past a traumatic experience. As the title implies, the book tells the story of what happens after "all the king's men" put Humpty Dumpty back together again. Humpty, an avid bird watcher, fell from his perch on a high wall, where he was sitting so he could be closer to the birds. After his injury, he was afraid of all heights and could only watch his beloved birds from the ground. To make himself feel better, he makes a perfect paper airplane that can soar through the air with the birds, but his airplane lands on the wall, and he works to overcome his fear and trauma so he can retrieve it:

> "I decided I was going to climb that wall.
> But the higher I got,
> the more nervous I felt.
> I didn't want to admit it:
> I was terrified.
> I didn't look up.
> I didn't look down.
> I just kept climbing.
> One step at a time . . .
> until I was no longer afraid."

The powerful self-management message of this text is that Humpty Dumpty heals at his own pace. The book portrays him sleeping on the floor because his loft bed is too high and not using a small ladder at the store to help him reach his favorite cereal because he is still afraid. For children who may have experienced traumas, both large and small, this book offers a starting place for thinking about the ways we experience and cope with trauma, and it provides hope that one day they can move beyond their fear and be like Humpty Dumpty, "the egg who got back up."

In reading this text, and others that address students' self-management and the emotion and cognitive Harvard domains, there is a clear connection to the CCR writing anchor standard 3: "Write narratives to develop real or imagined experiences or events using effective technique, well-chosen details and well-structured event sequences." The self-management competency focuses on how individuals regulate their thoughts, emotions, and behaviors as they react to an experience, which provides a strong starting place for children to write a narrative. Just as this text describes the series of events that happened after Humpty's fall, students can be asked to write (or draw) an experience from their life and how they managed it. Additionally, through the process of discussing how to write a beginning, middle, and end to a narrative, teachers can discuss an additional key SEL point: it is acceptable to have not reached "the end" yet, especially when dealing with a difficult experience. Just as Humpty Dumpty needed to allow himself time to heal both mentally and physically, it is important for children to hear that there is no timeline for moving past a traumatic event. For that reason, when they are writing their own narratives, their conclusions could either represent where they truly are in their recovery or perhaps detail where they aspire to be in the future.

Self-Management Book Suggestions

My Heart by Corinna Luyken (AD 320L)
After the Fall by Dan Santat (AD 550L)
Tidy by Emily Gravett (590L)

Social Awareness

The Good Egg by Jory John conveys the important message of finding a balance between taking care of yourself and taking care of your community. The story begins with the main character, the Good Egg, listing all of things the egg has done to help neighbors and friends, including trying to get its carton-mates to tame their unruly behavior. However, all of this focus on others exhausts the Good Egg, and it begins to crack, literally, under the pressure. After leaving the carton behind to find peace through recreation and relaxation, the egg heals and returns home, deciding to be kind to its fellow eggs, while prioritizing self-care. The Good Egg is welcomed back, and comments:

> "Here's what I realized:
> The other eggs aren't perfect,
> and I don't have to be either.
> I'm OK with that."

In addition to the clear connection to the self-management competency, this text also provides a powerful example of social awareness skills and the skills included in the social, values, and perspective Harvard domains. The Good Egg was so concerned about controlling others' behaviors that it damaged its own health. In understanding that others could be imperfect, the Good Egg reduced personal stress and allowed itself to create more positive relationships with others.

As students begin to develop their understanding of their own behavior in relation to others, which is at the heart of social awareness, they also begin to understand the concept of point of view. This is essential to addressing CCR reading anchor standard 6: "Assess how point of view or purpose shapes the content and style of a text." *The Good Egg*, for example, is written with first person narration, from the perspective of the Good Egg. In addition to identifying who the narrator is, in making connections to the SEL competency, students can also be guided as they begin to understand how this perspective shapes the story. They could consider how the story might be different if it were written from the point of view of one of the eggs that broke the rules. This consideration of alternate views can lead to fruitful discussions and writing activities in the classroom that support both the reading anchor standard and the SEL competency.

> ### Social Awareness Book Suggestions
>
> *Should I Share My Ice Cream?* by Mo Willems (260L)
> *The Good Egg* by Jory John (AD 510L)
> *What is Given From the Heart* by Patricia C. McKissack (AD 660L)

Relationship Skills

In *The Invisible Boy* by Trudy Ludwig, readers see the main character, Brian, move from a socially isolated outsider to a valued member of the class after he first befriends a new boy, and then is given the opportunity to demonstrate his art skills during a group activity. The illustrations support comprehension by providing a visual representation of Brian's evolution, showing Brian in black and white at the beginning of the book, and then adding more and more color as he is integrated into the friend groups in the classroom. Many students will likely be able to relate to Brian's feelings at the beginning of the book when he seems to be overlooked by everyone, including his classroom teacher, who is attending to the needs of more demanding children. He is also not included at recess when teams are chosen or invited to a classmate's birthday party.

This book provides a particularly powerful basis for conversations about the SEL competency of relationship skills as well as the social, perspectives, and identity Harvard domains. All students can be encouraged to practice perspective-taking, considering Brian's feelings when he was left out of the various peer groups, as well as the perspectives of Brian's classmates. Some of the students were truly unkind, while others may have been unaware of how Brian was feeling. As they consider the roles of the students in the story, they can think about how they might become more aware of who is included and who is excluded within their classroom and school, and brainstorm ways to make sure that all students in the school feel a sense of belonging.

This book and its focus on relationship skills allow for a powerful connection to CCR writing anchor standard 1: "Write arguments to support claims in an analysis of substantive topics or texts, using valid reasoning and relevant and sufficient evidence." As students are asked to discuss the various characters in *The Invisible Boy*, they will likely also be forming opinions about the characters' behaviors. Ideally, students will come to understand that there are many complexities in various relationships portrayed in the book. For example, students might want to critique the behavior of the teacher, but others could point out that Nathan and Sophie, the students drawing the teacher's attention away from Brian, need additional support from the teacher as they are learning the right ways to behave in the classroom. Others may point out that not every child can be invited to every birthday party, and therefore the children discussing the party at lunch were not intentionally causing Brian to feel left out. Finally, it is reasonable to assert that Brian could have been a little more outgoing, because once he reached out to the new student, he was able to begin to make friends. Each of these opinions can be supported with evidence from the text and would allow students to connect their personal experiences with ideas from the text as they describe their opinions about the book.

> **Relationship Skills Book Suggestions**
>
> *Nothing Rhymes with Orange* by Adam Rex (570L)
> *The Invisible Boy* by Trudy Ludwig (AD 680L)
> *The Day You Begin* by Jacqueline Woodson (AD 980L)

Responsible Decision-Making

The CASEL competency of responsible decision-making focuses on helping students understand how to make constructive choices and to consider the impact of their actions on themselves and others. *A Bike Like Sergio's* by Maribeth Boelts provides a strong fictional example for students to analyze and apply to their own lives. In this book, Ruben, the main character, wishes he could have a bike like his friend Sergio, but his family must spend their money on necessities. When he sees a woman drop what he thinks is $1 but is actually $100, he contemplates keeping it so he can buy a bike. When he finally decides to return it, the woman is grateful, and when he tells his family the story, they are proud. The book, however, reflects Ruben's honest feelings when he says:

"I am happy and mixed up,
full and empty, with what's
right and what's gone."

This book is a meaningful way to begin conversations with students about responsible decision-making and the cognitive, social, values, and perspective Harvard domains because it considers the complexities of Ruben's actions and emotions. When what Ruben thinks is a $1 bill first drops, Ruben picks it up, but does not go after the woman. He keeps the money, realizes that it is $100, and in the middle of the book has a moment of awareness of how the woman must feel when she thinks that she lost the money. He decides to return the money to her. However, even though he did the right thing, he feels conflicted because he no longer has the money or the possibility of buying a bike. This is a powerful message for students to come to understand; it is possible to have a variety of emotions, even when you have done the right thing.

In mapping Ruben's actions and thinking over the course of the text in order to understand his choices and feelings, students are also being taught to address CCR reading anchor standard 3: "Analyze how and why individuals, events, and ideas develop and interact over the course of a text." In the earliest grades, the focus is primarily on retelling the story, which would lead students to explain the series of events that led up to Ruben deciding to return the money. As students get older, however, they begin to focus more on the characters' feelings and motivations and how their actions contribute to the story. At this stage in the progression of the standards, students can be considering Ruben's actions as he moved from planning to keep the money so that he could buy a bike to realizing he needed to return it, even though it left him with conflicting emotions. This strengthens the connection to the responsible decision-making domain because it helps students see, in a fictionalized world, how decision-making can be complex.

> **Responsible Decision-Making Book Suggestions**
>
> *Stick and Stone* by Beth Ferry (250L)
> *A Bike Like Sergio's* by Maribeth Boelts (AD 540L)
> *Here Comes the Garbage Barge* by Jonah Winter (AD 670L)

The literary texts mentioned here and the informational texts identified in the next chapter all share one common characteristic: they were chosen because they move beyond simply telling an engaging story. Instead, alongside the story they tell, they share a message about how we want our students to participate in the world around them, including their classrooms, their homes, and their communities. With thoughtful integration, K-3 teachers can use the teaching of ELA, which has a prominent place in every school day, to also support students' social and emotional growth. This chapter and Chapter 8, which focuses on the use of informational texts, provide suggestions and ideas for beginning the thoughtful integration of ELA and SEL in the classroom.

LESSON PLAN

Title and Grade
What's In a Name? Understanding and Appreciating What Makes Us Unique Grade: K-1
Standards and Learning Objectives
Common Core Standard for ELA: Literary Text • CCSS.ELA-LITERACY.RL.1.2: Retell stories, including key details, and demonstrate understanding of their central message or lesson.

SEL Standard: CASEL
- Self-Awareness: The abilities to understand one's own emotions, thoughts, and values and how they influence behavior across contexts

SEL Standards: Harvard
- Emotion: Recognizing, expressing, and controlling your emotions as well as understanding and empathizing with others
- Values: Being a compassionate person who contributes to their community and world in positive ways
- Perspectives: Understanding how you view and approach the world, and how this view impacts how you see yourself and others
- Identity: Fostering an understanding of the diversity of identities within local and global communities

Learning Objectives
After listening to *The Name Jar* read aloud and participating in a variety of activities, the students will be able to retell the story and make a connection between their own feelings about the things that make them unique and the main character's experiences with her unique name.

ASSESSMENT

Students will be informally assessed on their understanding of the story through class discussions and the drawing/writing about the beginning, middle, and end of *The Name Jar*.

Students can be formally assessed on the activities completed from the choice board. The reading activity addressing beginning, middle, and end gives the students an opportunity to apply their knowledge of retelling a story to a new text. The social and emotional learning activity allows students to make connections between their own experiences and the experiences of the children in the books they read.

LEARNING PLAN
Instructional Resources and Materials
The Name Jar by Yangsook Choi
Additional books on the topic of names
Worksheet with boxes for the beginning, middle, and end of the story or blank paper
Lined paper and blank paper for word work activities
Copies of the first-grade choice board
Daily Plans
Stage 1: Group Activity (1 Day)
Ideally, parents or caregivers should be involved in the first day's activity several days before the group activity will be done in class. Prior to this activity, children should ask their parents or caregivers to tell them the story of how they got their name. If possible, the children can write or draw the key points from what they are told, but if that is not possible, the parents/caregivers can write a few words down to help the children remember. Once in class, the teacher can brainstorm some "interview" questions with the students. For example:
- How did you get your name?
- Do you like your name?
- If you weren't named _____, what would you like to be called?

After brainstorming questions, the students can pair up with a partner for an interview, with each partner having an opportunity to share his or her name story.

Stage 2: Read Aloud and Activities (2 Days)
This part of the lesson will have two different parts. On the first day, the teacher will read aloud *The Name Jar*, focusing on guiding the students to understand the story through a series of before, during, and after reading questions. The following questions provide some examples.
Before reading:
- What do you think this story is going to be about? Why do you think that? |

- What do you think the title means?
- What can you guess about the story by looking at the cover?

During reading:
- What do you think is going to happen next? How do you think the story will end?
- What are the pictures showing us about the story?
- Do you identify with Unhei? Why or why not?
- What do you think about how Unhei's classmates treated her? Do your thoughts change from the beginning to the end of the book?

After reading:
- Were you surprised that Unhei decided to keep her name? Why or why not?
- What is the main message of the story? (What do you think the author wanted us to learn?)
- What happened at the beginning, middle, and end of the story?
- What did you like or dislike about the story?

On day 2, the students will have a second exposure to the book. This can be differentiated to meet the needs of the class. Options include the teacher reading the book aloud to the whole class or a small group, students reading the book independently, with partners, or in small groups, and/or the use of an audio version of the book or video of someone reading the book from YouTube.

Based on the second reading of the story, and with teacher assistance if necessary, the students should draw pictures to represent what happened at the beginning, middle, and end of the story. Students, based on ability level, should be asked to write words or sentences to explain what is happening in their pictures. This will serve as a formative assessment of students' understanding of the progression of the story. If necessary, the teacher can begin class the next day with a review of key plot points.

Stage 3: Differentiated Learning (2–3 Days)
For the two to three days of this stage of the activity, the students should work through the choice-board activities. If the children are familiar with choice boards, and are able to work mostly independently, the teacher can use this time to pull small groups of students to provide assistance or challenge as needed. A sample choice board follows.

First-Grade Choice Board
Choose one activity from each category. Put an "x" in the box of the activity you completed.

Reading		
Choose one of the "name" books. Read it to yourself. Write or draw what happened at the beginning, middle, and end.	Choose one of the "name" books. Read it with a partner. Write or draw what happened at the beginning, middle, and end.	Choose one of the "name" books. Listen to it being read by the teacher or on YouTube. Write or draw what happened at the beginning, middle, and end.
Word Work		
Choose 2 words that you did not know from *The Name Jar* and 2 words that you did not know from the second "name" book. Use your context clues or a dictionary to figure out what the words mean. Fold a piece of paper into fourths, and draw a picture of each word. Write the word under the picture.	Practice saying and writing these words from *The Name Jar*. Make a second list with them in ABC order. • house • walk • would • thing • right • back • just	Practice saying and writing these words from *The Name Jar*. If you have time, make a list with them in ABC order. • the • it • was • and • she • your • red

Social and Emotional Learning		
You've read *The Name Jar* and at least one other book about someone's name. Write a short paragraph about how you feel about your name and how Unhei and the other character felt about their names.	Draw a picture showing how Unhei felt about her name at the end of the book. Draw a picture that shows how you feel about your name. Under each picture, write a sentence explaining your feelings.	Unhei had a unique name. Draw a picture of something that makes you unique. Under your picture, write this sentence, filling in the blanks: "I am unique because_____. Being unique makes me feel _____."

In addition to the choice board, this activity will require some additional books that focus on the topic of names. Some examples are:

- *My Name is Yoon* by Helen Recorvits (480L)
- *A Porcupine Named Fluffy* by Helen Lester (480L)
- *Alma and How She Got Her Name* by Juana Martinez-Neal (490L)
- *My Name Is Sangoel* by Karen Lynn Williams and Khadra Mohammed (AD 550L)
- *My Name Is Wakawakaloch!* by Chana Stiefel (AD 560L)
- *Change Your Name Store* by Leanne Shirtliffe (570L)
- *Chrysanthemum* by Kevin Henkes (570L)
- *My Name Is Bilal* by Asma Mobin-Uddin (570L)

Stage 4: Revisit Group Activity (1 Day)
This final day is an opportunity for students to share what they have learned during the differentiated learning time. Using the students' "beginning, middle, and end" reading papers from the differentiated reading activity, create groups or trios with children who read different books. Ask them to retell the story, focusing on what happened in the beginning, what happened in the middle, and what happened at the end.

Once this is complete, transition to a whole-group activity. Ask willing students to share their pictures and writing from the social and emotional learning activity. Conclude this lesson by asking the students questions such as:
- What have we learned about people's names? Why are names important?
- Is being unique a good thing or a bad thing? Why is it sometimes hard to be different?
- When was a time you felt different? How did people treat you? How would you like to be treated?

References

Choi, Y. (2001). *The name jar* (Y. Choi, Illus.). Dragonfly Books.
Henkes, K. (1991). *Chrysanthemum* (K. Henkes, Illus.). Greenwillow Books.
Lester, H. (1989). *A porcupine named Fluffy* (L. Munsinger, Illus.). Houghton Mifflin.
Martinez-Neal, J. (2018). *Alma and how she got her name* (J. Martinez-Neal, Illus.). Candlewick.
Recorvits, H. (2003). *My name is Yoon* (G. Swiatkowska, Illus.). Frances Foster Books.
Shirtliffe, L. (2014). *Change your name store* (T. Kügler, Illus.). Sky Pony.
Stiefel, C. (2019). *My name Is Wakawakaloch!* (M. Sullivan, Illus.). Clarion Books.
Uddin-Mobin, A. (2005). *My name is Bilal* (B. Kiwak, Illus.). Boyds Mills Press.
Williams, K. L., & Mohammed, K. (2009). *My name is Sangoel* (C. Stock, Illus.). Eerdmans Books for Young Readers.

References

Hoffman, J. L., Teale, W. H., & Yokota, J. (2015). The book matters! Choosing complex narrative texts to support literacy discussions. *Young Children, 70*(4), 8–15.
National Governors Association Center for Best Practices & Council of Chief State School Officers. (2010). *Common core state standards for English language arts and literacy in history/social studies, science, and technical subjects*. Authors.

Book List

Boelts, M. (2016). *A bike like Sergios* (N. Z. Jones, Illus.). Candlewick Press.
Cherry, M. A. (2019). *Hair love* (V. Harrison, Illus.). Kokila.
Choi, Y. (2001). *The name jar* (Y. Choi, Illus.). Dragonfly Books.
Deacon, A. (2015). *I am Henry Finch* (V. Schwarz, Illus.). Candlewick Press.
Ferry, B. (2015). *Stick and stone* (T. Lichtenheld, Illus.). Clarion Books.
Gravett, E. (2017). *Tidy* (E. Gravett, Illus.). Simon & Schuster Books for Young Readers.
John, J. (2019). *The good egg* (P. Oswald, Illus.). HarperCollins Children's Books.
Kelkar, S. (2019). *The many colors of Harpreet Singh* (A. Marley, Illus.). Sterling Children's Books.
Love, J. (2018). *Julián is a mermaid* (J. Love, Illus.). Candlewick Press.
Ludwig, T. (2013). *The invisible boy* (P. Barton, Illus.). Alfred A. Knopf.
Luyken, C. (2019). *My heart* (C. Luyken, Illus.). Dial Books.
McKissack, P. C. (2019). *What is given from the heart* (A. Harrison, Illus.). Schwartz & Wade Books.
Rex, A. (2017). *Nothing rhymes with orange* (A. Rex, Illus.). Chronicle Books.
Santat, D. (2017). *After the fall: How Humpty Dumpty got back up again* (D. Santat, Illus.). Roaring Book Press.
Willems, M. (2011). *Should I share my ice cream?* (M. Willems, Illus.). Hyperion Books for Children.
Williams, K. L., & Mohammed, K. (2009). *My name is Sangoel* (C. Stock, Illus.). Eerdmans Books for Young Readers.
Winter, J. (2010). *Here comes the garbage barge* (Red Nose Studio, Illus.). Schwartz & Wade Books.
Woodson, J. (2018). *The day you begin* (R. López, Illus.). Nancy Paulsen Books.

8

Integrating SEL and ELA Using Informational Texts

Thoughtfully chosen informational texts have a powerful role to play in mixed-ability early elementary classrooms. Not only do they allow all students to develop the English Language Arts (ELA) skills needed to comprehend increasingly complex informational texts in a variety of content areas, skills that will be essential as they progress through school, but they also provide an opportunity for them to build their social and emotional competencies. In addition, explicit instruction in reading informational texts can provide students an opportunity to learn the skills necessary to delve deeply into a topic of interest at the same time they are gaining opportunities to explore the complex content they crave.

As noted in Chapter 7, the Common Core State Standards (CCSS) provide a framework for literacy instruction that is broad enough to allow for connections across the academic curriculum, as well as the integration of additional competencies such as those related to social and emotional learning (SEL). Instruction using informational texts, in particular biographies and other narrative nonfiction, provides an invaluable opportunity for teachers to bring in SEL competencies into daily classroom lessons. The insights provided into the struggles and successes of real people, many of whom are familiar to the students, allow students to see connections between their own lives and the lives of the people portrayed in the texts. These texts provide authentic examples of how people may struggle with demonstrating SEL skills, but ultimately, in most cases, they show growth.

In ELA instruction, the CCSS emphasize the use of informational texts because as students get older, they will be required to read increasingly challenging texts in the content areas and to write in a variety of genres, including those that are modeled by the informational texts they read. For the youngest readers, those in grades K-3, educators are expected to include a wide range of informational texts so that students can develop the content and vocabulary knowledge necessary for success in later grades. Wixson and Valencia (2014) note that this reading "becomes the foundation, or the background knowledge (of the world and the words), students need to comprehend increasingly substantive, 'meaty' content texts as they move from grade to grade" (p. 432). Similarly, this background knowledge "of the world and the words" will also support their writing development. While some of the texts and lesson ideas used in this chapter will have connections to the texts and content standards addressed in Chapters 5 and 6, the focus in those chapters was on integrating SEL with science, technology, engineering, and math (STEM), and social studies, using picture books. This chapter will also use informational texts, but it will focus on the integration of ELA standards with the teaching of SEL.

The exciting, and challenging, issue with integrating SEL with ELA is that SEL can be connected to just about any standard you are addressing. Are you working on having your students ask and answer questions about the text, using text-based evidence to support their answers? Add in some questions about how the individuals were feeling or why they behaved in a certain way. Are you working with students to build fluency in their read-alouds? Use texts where the individuals explicitly address their emotions or describe working through problems. Are your students working to develop their vocabulary? Consider having them list the different ways individuals' emotions are described in the text. Because there are so many possibilities for integrating SEL with ELA, this chapter will focus on the closest connections and the most powerful opportunities for integration. It is our intention, however, that these ideas should only serve as a starting point for your thinking.

Table 8.1 provides the anchor standard, relevant CCSS for the early elementary grades, and suggested Collaborative for Academic, Social, and Emotional Learning (CASEL) competencies and Harvard domains that could be integrated with the grade-level standards. The four specific grade-level standards are included because they help guide thinking and planning for differentiation. If there are gaps in students' knowledge, or if students need additional guidance to meet the grade-level standard, begin by looking at standards from earlier years. If students are in need of additional challenge, consider bringing in some of the expectations from higher grades.

Table 8.1 Sample Common Core State Standards and Related SEL Competencies

Sample CCSS Anchor Standard	Specific Grade-Level Standards	SEL Competencies and Domains
Reading Standard 3 Analyze how and why individuals, events, and ideas develop and interact over the course of a text.	Informational Texts • Kindergarten: With prompting and support, describe the connection between two individuals, events, ideas, or pieces of information in a text. • First grade: Describe the connection between two individuals, events, ideas, or pieces of information in a text. • Second grade: Describe the connection between a series of historical events, scientific ideas or concepts, or steps in technical procedures in a text. • Third grade: Describe the relationship between a series of historical events, scientific ideas or concepts, or steps in technical procedures in a text, using language that pertains to time, sequence, and cause/effect.	Social awareness Social Values Perspectives
Reading Standard 6 Assess how point of view or purpose shapes the content and style of a text.	Informational Texts • Kindergarten: Name the author and illustrator of a text, and define the role of each in presenting the ideas or information in a text. • First Grade: Distinguish between information provided by pictures or other illustrations and information provided by the words in a text. • Second grade: Identify the main purpose of a text, including what the author wants to answer, explain, or describe. • Third grade: Distinguish their own point of view from that of the author of a text.	Self-management Emotion Cognitive

Sample CCSS Anchor Standard	Specific Grade-Level Standards	SEL Competencies and Domains
Reading Standard 8 Delineate and evaluate the argument and specific claims in a text, including the validity of the reasoning as well as the relevance and sufficiency of the evidence.	*Informational Texts* • *Kindergarten*: With prompting and support, identify the reasons an author gives to support points in a text. • *First Grade*: Identify the reasons an author gives to support points in a text. • *Second Grade*: Describe how reasons support specific points the author makes in a text. • *Third Grade*: Describe the logical connection between particular sentences and paragraphs in a text (e.g., comparison, cause/effect, first/second/third in a sequence).	Relationship skills Social Perspectives Identity

Writing Standard 1 Write arguments to support claims in an analysis of substantive topics or texts, using valid reasoning and relevant and sufficient evidence.	• *Kindergarten*: Use a combination of drawing, dictating, and writing to compose opinion pieces in which students tell a reader the topic or the name of the book they are writing about and state an opinion or preference about the topic or book (e.g., My favorite book is . . .).
	• *First grade*: Write opinion pieces in which they introduce the topic or name the book they are writing about, state an opinion, supply a reason for the opinion, and provide some sense of closure.
	• *Second grade*: Write opinion pieces in which they introduce the topic or book they are writing about, state an opinion, supply reasons that support the opinion, use linking words (e.g., *because, and, also*) to connect opinion and reasons, and provide a concluding statement or section.
	• *Third grade*: Write opinion pieces on topics or texts, supporting a point of view with reasons.
	  a. Introduce the topic or text they are writing about, state an opinion, and create an organizational structure that lists reasons.
	  b. Provide reasons that support the opinion.
	  c. Use linking words and phrases (e.g., *because, therefore, since, for example*) to connect opinion and reasons.
	  d. Provide a concluding statement or section.
		Responsible decision-making Cognitive Social Values Perspectives

(Continued)

Table 8.1 (Continued)

Sample CCSS Anchor Standard	Specific Grade-Level Standards	SEL Competencies and Domains

Writing Standard 3 Write narratives to develop real or imagined experiences or events using effective technique, well-chosen details, and well-structured event sequences.	• *Kindergarten*: Use a combination of drawing, dictating, and writing to narrate a single event or several loosely linked events, tell about the events in the order in which they occurred, and provide a reaction to what happened.
	• *First grade*: Write narratives in which they recount two or more appropriately sequenced events, include some details regarding what happened, use temporal words to signal event order, and provide some sense of closure.
	• *Second grade*: Write narratives in which they recount a well-elaborated event or short sequence of events; include details to describe actions, thoughts, and feelings; use temporal words to signal event order; and provide a sense of closure.
	• *Third grade*: Write narratives to develop real or imagined experiences or events using effective technique, descriptive details, and clear event sequences.
	  a. Establish a situation and introduce a narrator and/or characters; organize an event sequence that unfolds naturally.
	  b. Use dialogue and descriptions of actions, thoughts, and feelings to develop experiences and events or show the response of characters to situations.
	  c. Use temporal words and phrases to signal event order.
	  d. Provide a sense of closure.
		Self-awareness Emotion Cognitive

The following section focuses on biographies and other narrative nonfiction texts that can serve as exemplars for integrating SEL with the ELA CCSS. While there are innumerable quality children's books available, we found these both engaging and useful for supporting learning in both SEL and ELA.

Text Exemplars

Picture book biographies and other narrative nonfiction can play an important role in both the teaching of ELA and the development of social and emotional competencies. Morgan (2009), for example, notes that picture book biographies are particularly beneficial in early elementary classrooms because they represent various diverse groups, they can be inspirational to children of all ages, they are preferred over textbooks, and, when written carefully, they present accurate information on people from different cultural backgrounds in ways that are free of bias. In considering the unique needs of young, gifted BIPOC children, authors have also pointed out the important role biographies can play in connecting culturally diverse students to the classroom curriculum, helping them see themselves as individuals with high potential and providing images of people who are able to achieve, despite experiencing significant hardships. These books are also valuable for all children, because they provide examples of how people from diverse backgrounds have strengths that will allow them to succeed and make positive contributions to society (Abellán-Pagnani & Hébert, 2013; Floyd & Hébert, 2010). Like biographies, narrative nonfiction tells a "real" story about people and events but with a slightly different focus. Rather than detailing the life journey of a single person, narrative nonfiction may focus on more than one person, or on topics that expand beyond one individual's life.

Self-Awareness

It Began with a Page: Gyo Fujikawa Drew the Way, written by Kyo Maclear, is an example of a picture book that straddles the boundary between narrative nonfiction and biography. While the text focuses primarily on the life of Gyo Fujikawa, it also includes references to her family and their experiences in Japanese internment camps during World War II. The books describes Fujikawa's development as an artist, beginning with her drawing a picture as a five-year-old. As a female and an Asian in the United States during the early 20th century, she is portrayed as an outsider, both in school and college. The text notes, however, that she also did not feel a sense of belonging in traditional Japanese art schools when she moved there as an adult, so she chose to travel throughout the country learning on her own. Upon her return to the United States prior to World Word II, she found work as an artist in New York. A strength of this book is the authentic but still child-friendly way the book addresses Fujikawa's emotions when her family was forced into internment camps. It notes that she felt "tiny and terrible" and that "no pictures would come." However, it also says that eventually:

> "She drew to keep her worries still and to save money her family would need. When angry strangers saw her as the enemy, her drawing comforted her. When the world felt gray, color lifted her."

The text continues to tell Fujikawa's story, describing how she fought against prejudices in the 1960s by writing and drawing a book featuring babies from various ethnic backgrounds. When a publisher balked at publishing an "integrated" book when so much of the United States was still segregated, the book notes that she said to the publisher: "It shouldn't be that way. Not out there in the streets. Not here on this page. We need to break the rules."

This book is particularly powerful for teaching the SEL competency of self-awareness and considering the Harvard domains of emotions, values, perspectives, and identity. It acknowledges Fukijawa's strong negative emotions when her family was in an internment camp, but it also provides an explanation of how she was able to use her art as a coping strategy. Additionally, she drew upon her feelings during that time when she fought to have her picture book published. The note from the author and the illustrator at the end of the text also provides additional insight into Fujikawa's other fights for justice, including challenging traditional gender roles and fighting for labor rights.

This text and the SEL competencies and domains also support a strong connection to the CCSS anchor standard 3: "Write narratives to develop real or imagined experiences or events using effective technique, well-chosen details and well-structured event sequences." Fujikawa's life experience provides a model because she experienced hardship, found ways to manage that hardship, and used her experiences to guide her life moving forward. Students can use this text, and others that address characters and emotions, as a starting place for writing about their own emotions. Beginning with Fukijawa's experiences, they can consider difficult experiences from their own lives at the same time they are identifying how they can manage their feelings and what they might learn from the experience.

Self-Awareness Book Suggestions

Be the Change: A Grandfather Gandhi Story by Arun Gandhi & Bethany Hegedus (610L)
It Began With a Page: How Gyo Fujikawa Drew the Way by Kyo Maclear (700L)*
Soldier for Equality: Jose De La Luz Saenz And The Great War by Duncan Tonatiuh (860L)

*This is an approximate level, as a definitive measure is not available.

Self-Management

Like *It Began With a Page*, *The Important Thing About Margaret Wise Brown* by Mac Barnett addresses issues related to understanding and regulating emotions in a child-friendly way. This book describes the life of the author of such classic children's books as *The Important Book*, *Runaway Bunny*, and *Goodnight Moon*. While appropriate for all children, this book may appeal particularly to those for whom Brown's books played a role in their earliest literacy experiences. The text borrows phrases from *The Important Book* (e.g., "The important thing about . . ." and "It is true . . .") and, as with all great picture books, draws readers in with images as well as text. The illustrations in this book include the covers of some of Brown's most famous books, and the illustrator has created visuals that, in many cases, look like they could have come from one of Brown's collaborators.

In addition to these engaging factors, the text also breaks the "fourth wall," or the boundary between the text and the reader. Frequently, the author asks questions of the reader about the key ideas in the text:

> "And isn't it important that children's books
> contain the things children think of
> and the things children do,
> even if those things seem strange?"

This technique may be a curiosity for young readers, but in addition to drawing them in, it also serves to focus attention on key themes in the text. For example, the previous quote sets up the readers to understand that Brown's books were often rejected because they did not follow the traditional norms of the children's publishing world. Broadly, this book focuses on Margaret Wise Brown's distinctiveness in her life and in the books she wrote. While the author points out some of the strange things she did (e.g., swimming naked in cold water, building a door in her house that led out to a cliff, and buying an entire cart full of flowers after she received her first payment for a book), it was the uniqueness of her books that provided the conflict in the biography of her life. Because a librarian at the New York Public Library did not see the value in Brown's nontraditional children's books, the books were not purchased for use at that library, or other libraries where the staff respected the opinion of this one librarian.

It is in this consideration of Brown's distinctiveness and the conflict between Brown and the librarian that the SEL components are found. First, a key theme is that difference should be celebrated, not ignored or hidden. It describes some of the "strange" things that Brown did as both a child and adult, and makes an explicit connection to how some of those strange things influenced her books. It also makes clear that Brown was both embraced by her friends and successful as a children's book author despite some of these oddities and the rejection of some establishment librarians. Second, the text describes how Brown, when she was not invited to a social event for authors and illustrators at the New York Public Library, set up her own tea party on the steps of the library with her book editor. Both characteristics of the text address the CASEL competency of self-management and the emotion and cognitive Harvard domains. Brown's eccentricities were positive for her and never bothersome or hurtful to anyone else. Students can discuss how Brown must have felt at different points in her life and consider how the defiant act of setting up her own celebration on the library steps may have helped her address her feelings as well as serve as an appropriate act of defiance when faced with rejection.

The SEL competency of self-management also frequently aligns with the CCSS anchor standard 6: "Assess how point of view or purpose shapes the content and style of a text." In the elementary grades, this standard focuses on students understanding the key purpose of a text, and later, understanding their own and the author's point of view. In this text, and in many examples of literary nonfiction and biographies for youth, the main purpose of the text is to describe how an individual overcame difficulties. As students come to understand this key purpose, they are also addressing ideas related to the SEL competency of self-management.

Self-Management Book Suggestions

Brave Ballerina: The Story of Janet Collins by Michelle Meadows (570L)
The Important Thing About Margaret Wise Brown by Mac Barnett (620L)
Emmanuel's Dream: The True Story of Emmanuel Ofosu Yeboah by Laurie Ann Thomson (AD 770L)

Social Awareness
One of the engaging characteristics of *The Important Thing About Margaret Wise Brown* is that it provides a previously unknown look at an author who is likely familiar to many students. *Carter Reads the Newspaper* by Deborah Hopkinson is a traditional picture book biography that engages students by following a somewhat similar formula.

Unlike some biographies for children that tell the life stories of famous people who might be found in a textbook, or familiar people from popular culture, this book hooks students by telling the story of the unfamiliar person behind a familiar remembrance, Black History Month. The first half of the book tells the story of Carter's struggles as a young person born ten years after the end of the Civil War. His parents instilled in him a sense of pride in who they were and an understanding of the importance of being informed citizens. The second half of the book traces Carter's evolution from a young man struggling to make money and continue to learn while working in the coalmines, to his graduation with his PhD from Harvard University and his work to establish Negro History Week, which eventually became Black History Month.

This book provides a powerful example of social awareness, as well as the social, values, and perspective Harvard domains. Although Carter was born to formerly enslaved people, could only attend school 4 months a year when he was young, and had to drop out of school before high school to earn money, he was able to find resources in his community to support his learning. He was also able to work within existing systems to get his degrees, eventually becoming the first and only Black American whose parents had been enslaved to receive a doctorate in history. As the students read this text they can discuss the ways Carter managed his difficult situations (e.g., going to bed early on Saturday so his mother could wash his only pair of clothes before church, reading newspapers that had been used to wrap food, finding a community of learners to support his desire for information). They can also come to realize how the people in his life served as both supports and sources of challenge. For example, when one of Carter's professors suggested Black people had no history, Carter did not argue; he used his education to create a different narrative. The text explains:

> "At Harvard, so the story goes, one of Carter's professors said that Black people had no history. . . . Carter spoke up. "No people lacked a history," he said. The professors challenged Carter to prove him wrong. For the rest of his life, Carter did just that."

This text and the social awareness CASEL competency also provide a strong connection to the CCSS ELA anchor standard 6: "Analyze how and why individuals, events, and ideas develop and interact over the course of a text," which, in the early elementary grades focuses on making connections between people and events in a text. As students address the resources and supports that were an important part of Carter's life, they are also addressing the social awareness competency and describing the connections and relationships that are the primary focus of CCSS anchor standard 6.

Social Awareness Book Suggestions

The Watcher: Jane Goodall's Life with the Chimps by Jeanette Winter (AD 630L)
Carter Reads the Newspaper by Deborah Hopkinson (810L)
Separate is Never Equal: Sylvia Mendez & Her Family's Fight for Desegregation by Duncan Tonatiuh (AD 870L)

Relationship Skills

Early in the text *Wilma's Way Home: The Life of Wilma Mankiller* by Doreen Rappaport, the author references *Gadugi*, the Cherokee philosophy of helping each other. This philosophy is evident throughout the book as Mankiller looks for the relationships with native people that can sustain her. After being moved from Oklahoma to San Francisco as a result of a relocation program, Mankiller first turns to the community resources near her home in California to help her understand her heritage, but she eventually moves back to Cherokee communities in Oklahoma, where she worked with the Cherokee Nation government to make things better for indigenous people. Throughout the text, the main theme is people helping one another to achieve their goals. For example, the text states:

> "Wilma . . . believed that
> the Cherokee people of Bell [Oklahoma] knew best
> what they need to do to better their lives."

The power of relationships is demonstrated when the people decided they needed running water, and, after receiving a grant, they worked together to plan the project and lay the pipes. This project encouraged the Cherokee people to "believe they had the power to change their lives." Throughout the book, there are numerous other references to the importance of relationships, including the elders who taught Mankiller about Cherokee traditions in California, the friends and family who cared for her when she was in a serious car accident, and members of the Cherokee Nation who supported her when she ran for office and eventually became the first woman chief of the Cherokee Nation.

These numerous examples of *Gadugi* also provide a powerful example of the relationship skills CASEL competency and the social, perspectives, and identity Harvard domains, while allowing for integration with CCSS anchor standard 8: "Delineate and evaluate the argument and specific claims in a text, including the validity of the reasoning as well as the relevance and sufficiency of the evidence." In this text, and in many picture books that support the teaching of relationship skills, there will be numerous examples of how a relationship was developed and supported. As teachers and students consider the life of Wilma Mankiller, they can begin with the key philosophy of *Gadugi*, and look for the specific examples from the text that show this philosophy being demonstrated in Mankiller's life.

Relationship Skills Book Suggestions

Rescue and Jessica: A Life-Changing Friendship by Jessica Kensky & Patrick Downes (550L)
Sit-in: How Four Friends Stood Up by Sitting Down by Andrea Davis Pinkney (600L)
Wilma's Way Home: The Life of Wilma Mankiller by Doreen Rappaport (840L)

Responsible Decision-Making

Another biography appropriate for integrating SEL with teaching ELA is *Our House is on Fire: Greta Thunberg's Call to Save the Planet* by Jeanette Winter. Of note is that this text is at approximately the same Lexile level as the Margaret Wise Brown biography, but because it is shorter, it may be more appropriate for younger readers or less proficient readers in the K-3 grade band. The book uses many of Greta's own words, including her noting that as a young child she felt "invisible." It traces Greta's awakening to the crisis of climate change, and, because she felt powerless to make a difference, her resulting depression. The book revisits the idea of feeling "invisible" as she began her climate strike and felt ignored, but then tells readers: "The quiet girl who always felt invisible was asked to speak to very important people at the United Nations climate talks in Poland." The book ends on an empowering note. It explains that Greta's protests led to a worldwide children's movement and calls upon children to consider what they can do to make a difference.

The value of this book is three-fold. First, neurodivergent students like Greta may find comfort in seeing their struggles depicted on the page in a way that acknowledges them but does not focus on them as a limiting factor or as a defining characteristic. Second, this book can be particularly powerful for gifted students who may be aware of issues like climate change earlier than their same-age peers. It acknowledges how this awareness can change a child's life, and how difficult it can be when children feel powerless to make an impact. The book states that Greta thought:

> "What use is school without a future?
> What can I do, she wondered."

While Greta's advocacy focuses on climate change, this message is an important one for all students to hear. They may feel powerless to make a difference, but identifying small changes they can make at school or in their local communities can help empower them. Finally, this book is valuable because it provides a strong example of the SEL competency of responsible decision-making, and the cognitive social, values, and perspectives Harvard domain. The responsible decision-making competency focuses on whether an individual made good decisions and what the impact of those decisions was. For students who have been taught that going to school is important, the idea of missing school to start a climate strike might be problematic. Others may think that it was acceptable because of the enormity of the problem. In class, with teacher guidance, students can discuss whether or not Greta's climate strike was an example of responsible decision-making, and they can use this discussion as a beginning place for their writing.

The CASEL competency of responsible decision-making ties in particularly well with the ELA anchor writing standard 1: "Write arguments to support claims in an analysis of substantive topics or texts, using valid reasoning and relevant and sufficient evidence." Inherent in any consideration of responsible decision-making is the question of whether or not a decision was truly responsible. Students can express an opinion and use evidence from the text and their own experiences to write increasingly complex opinion pieces.

Responsible Decision-Making Book Suggestions

Our House is on Fire: Greta Thunberg's Call to Save the Planet by Jeanette Winter (680L)
Brave Girl: Clara and the Shirtwaist Makers' Strike of 1909 by Michelle Markel (AD 760L)
A Time to Act: John F. Kennedy's Big Speech by Shana Corey (AD 850L)

Throughout this chapter and in Chapter 7, the focus has been on teaching specific SEL skills with ELA CCSS, and these connections are clear and strong. However, it can also be instructive to take a broader look at the totality of the books used here and in previous chapters. By including books by and about people from different racial and ethnic backgrounds—English learners, those from a variety of socio-economic statuses, and those with disabilities—all children in a classroom should be able to recognize themselves in the texts that are being shared, and all children can see that their classmates are unique, talented individuals with something to contribute both to their classroom and to broader society. This message is at least as important as the individual SEL domains and CCSS addressed in the planned lessons.

LESSON PLAN

Title and Grade
What Do You Do When Your "House is on Fire"? Reflecting on Greta Thunberg's Decisions Grade: 2 or 3
Standards and Learning Objectives
Common Core Standard for ELA: Writing • CCSS.ELA-Literacy.W.2.1: Write opinion pieces in which they introduce the topic or book they are writing about, state an opinion, supply reasons that support the opinion, use linking words (e.g., *because, and, also*) to connect opinion and reasons, and provide a concluding statement or section. **SEL Standard: CASEL** • Responsible decision-making: The abilities to make caring and constructive choices about personal behavior and social interactions across diverse situations **SEL Standards: Harvard** • Cognitive: Problem-solving, working through challenges, task initiation and task management • Social: Accurately interpreting others' behavior, effectively negotiating social situations, and interacting positively with others • Values: Being a compassionate person who contributes to their community and world in positive ways • Perspectives: Understanding how you view and approach the world, and how this view impacts how you see yourself and others

Learning Objectives

After listening to *Our House is on Fire* read aloud and participating in a variety of activities, the students will write short opinion pieces explaining whether they believe Greta Thunberg's climate strike was a responsible decision.

ASSESSMENT

Informal assessment will include assessment of students' participation in whole- and small-group discussions and completion of the daily activities.

Students' opinion piece should be assessed formally using a rubric. Teachers may use a common rubric, such as the one used for the "6+1 Traits of Writing" or a teacher-created rubric that includes key criteria such as:
- Purpose (or argument/thesis)
- Organization
- Evidence (reasons)
- Conventions

LEARNING PLAN

Instructional Resources and Materials

Our House is On Fire: Greta Thunberg's Call to Save the Planet by Jeanette Winter
Short clip from *Toy Story, Luca,* or another movie/television show
Note cards with "What would you do?" questions
Decision-making steps note sheet
Chart paper
Additional books on Greta Thunberg and/or links to videos/podcasts
Lined paper and/or Post-it notes for note taking
Story frame or sentence starters to support the writing of opinion pieces
Assessment rubric for opinion piece

Daily Plans

Stage 1: Group Activity (1 Day)
Begin with a short clip from a movie that shows a character bullying or acting badly toward another child. Sid from *Toy Story* (1995) is a classic example, and Ercole Visconti from the 2021 film *Luca* is a more recent example. Engage the students in a conversation about how the characters could respond. Lead the students through a version of responsible decision-making steps such as these:
1. Define the problem or the decision to be made.
2. Brainstorm a list of options/solutions.
3. Consider the consequences of each option/solution.
4. Make a decision.
5. Evaluate the results and reflect.

After completing the introductory discussion, ask small groups of children to consider "What Would You Do?" questions. For example:
- There is a new student in your class who is sitting by herself at lunch while you are sitting with your friends. What would you do?
- You find $20 on the ground at recess. What would you do?
- A good friend tells you his parents are fighting a lot at home and that it makes him upset, but he asks you not to tell anyone. What would you do?

Stage 2: Read Aloud and Activities (2 Days)
Read aloud *Our House is on Fire: Greta Thunberg's Call to Save the Planet* to the class. Using the CROWD strategy described in Chapter 4, or another format to guide your development of discussion questions, ask students a variety of questions that allow them to develop their understanding of the key points in the text, including those that are directly stated and those that must be inferred.
- Completion: Greta Thunberg was concerned about _____.

- **Recall:** What happened when Greta first found out about climate change?
- **Open-ended:** Do you think Greta's climate strike was a good idea? Why or why not? Why do you think Greta says: "Our house is on fire"?
- **W's:** Who taught Greta about climate change? What did she do to try to get people to pay attention to climate change? Where did Greta speak to large, adult audiences about climate change? When did her individual protest become something more? Why was Greta depressed after learning about climate change?
- **Distancing:** What have you heard about in the news that has made you upset or concerned? What others books have we read that show a child or a young person trying to make a difference? What are some things you could do to help address climate change or another problem you see?

On the second day of this stage, small groups of students will re-read *Our House is on Fire*, this time focusing on the decision-making steps. If needed, students can work with the teacher or teaching assistant, or listen to an audio version of the story. They can either be given a piece of paper to document their thinking, or they can discuss and share their discussion with the whole class. Questions could include:

- What was the problem Greta was trying to address?
- What were some of the other options for dealing with the problem?
- What were the pros and cons of each option?
- What option did she choose?
- What were the results, both positive and negative, of that choice?

After students share their ideas, the teacher can conclude this stage by asking the students to brainstorm a list of questions they still have about Greta Thunberg. These questions should be written on large sheets of paper and posted in a visible place.

Stage 3: Differentiated Learning (2–3 Days)
On day 1 of this stage, ask the students to learn more about Greta Thunberg by reading texts and listening to media, endeavoring to answer some of the questions posed in class the previous day. On days 2 and 3 of this stage, students will plan for and write a piece where they state and defend their opinion on whether or not Greta Thunberg made a responsible decision by engaging in a climate strike. If students have not been introduced to opinion writing, an additional day may be necessary for the teacher to discuss the components, perhaps doing a shared writing activity with the class to create an opinion piece on another topic.

Learners' individual needs will be met through differentiation of content, process, and product.

Content:
Students are given choices of books and/or multimedia.
- Articles from Newsela adjusted to meet students' reading levels
- Greta Thunberg's TED talk
- *Greta Thunberg: Teen Climate Activist* by Rachel Rose (440L)
- *Greta Thunberg* by Katlin Sarantou (AD520L)
- *Fighting Climate Change with Greta Thunberg* by Kristy Stark (760L)
- *Who is Greta Thunberg?* by Jill Leonard (910L)
- *Greta's story: The Schoolgirl Who Went on Strike to Save the Planet* by Valentina Camerini (980L)
- Chapters or sections from books such as *We are Power: How Nonviolent Activism Changes the World* by Todd Hasak-Lowy

Process:
Students can choose how to document their additional learning on Greta Thunberg. They can write brief statements on Post-it notes and attach them to the relevant question on the chart paper. They can create a two-column notes form,

with the question on one side and their learning on another. Teachers can also differentiate processes by giving students the choice to work individually or with a partner. The teacher or teaching assistant can also work with a small group to provide support or to guide students who could benefit from additional challenge.

Product:
For the writing, students in need of assistance can be provided a writing frame for opinion pieces that provides sentence starters and a clear structure. Students who could benefit from a challenge could be asked to integrate information from more than one source or to include a rebuttal to a common argument, (e.g., "Some people might argue that Greta should have stayed in school so she could learn the skills to combat climate change, but I believe . . ."). Students can also meet with a teacher or teaching assist to provide additional support. Additional accommodations can include text-to-speech software, translation dictionaries, and the option for submitting a verbal response if necessary.

Stage 4: Revisit Group Activity (1 Day)
On the first day, students were introduced to a decision-making framework and "What would you do?" questions. On this final day, students can identify a problem they see in their home, school, or community and brainstorm ways to address it using the decision-making framework. Throughout the school year, this could become the basis for a class project or a method for addressing issues of concern within the school.

References

Camerini, V. (2019). *Greta's story: The schoolgirl who went on strike to save the planet.* (V. Carratello, Illus.). Alladin.

Casarosa, E. (Director). (2021). *Luca* [Film]. Pixar Animation Studios.

Hasak-Lowy, T. (2020). *We are power: How nonviolent activism changes the world.* Harry N. Abrams.

Lasseter, J. (Director). (1995). *Toy story* [Film]. Pixar Animation Studios.

Leonard, J. (2020). *Who is Greta Thunberg?* (M. Gutierrez, Illus.) Penguin Workshop.
Rose, R. (2020). *Greta Thunberg: Teen climate activist.* Bearcub Books.
Sarantou, K. (2021). *Greta Thunberg* (J. Bane, Illus.) Cherry Lake Publishing.
Stark, K. (2020). *Fighting climate change with Greta Thunberg.* Full Tilt Press.

References

Abellán-Pagnani, L., & Hébert, T. P. (2013). Using picture books to guide and inspire young gifted Hispanic students. *Gifted Child Today, 36*(1), 47–56. https://doi.org/10.1177/1076217512459735

Floyd, E. F., & Hébert, T. P. (2010). Using picture book biographies. *Gifted Child Today, 33*(2), 38–46.

Morgan, H. (2009). Picture book biographies for young children: A way to teach multiple perspectives. *Early Childhood Education Journal, 37*(3), 219–227. https://doi.org/10.1007/s10643-009-0339-7

Wixson, K. K., & Valencia, S. W. (2014). CCSS-ELA suggestions and cautions for addressing text complexity. *Reading Teacher, 67*(6), 430–434.

Book List

Barnett, M. (2019). *The important thing about Margaret Wise Brown* (S. Jacoby, Illus.). Balzer + Bray.

Corey, S. (2017). *A time to act: John F. Kennedy's big speech* (R. G. Christie, Illus.). NorthSouth Books.

Gandhi, A., & Hegedus, B. (2016). *Be the change: A grandfather Gandhi story* (E. Turk, Illus.). Antheneum Books for Young Readers.

Hopkinson, D. (2018). *Carter reads the newspaper* (D. Tate, Illus.). Peachtree.

Kensky, J., & Downes, P. (2018). *Rescue & Jessica: A life-changing friendship* (S. Magoon, Illus.). Candlewick Press.

Maclear, K. (2019). *It began with a page: How Gyo Fujikawa drew the way* (J. Morstand, Illus.). Harper.

Markel, M. (2013). *Brave girl: Clara and the shirtwaist makers' strike of 1909* (M. Sweet, Illus.). Balzer + Bray.

Meadows, M. (2019). *Brave ballerina: The story of Janet Collins* (E. Glenn, Illus.). Henry Holt and Co.

Pickney, A. D. (2010). *Sit-in: How four friends stood up by sitting down* (B. Pinkney, Illus.). Little, Brown and Company.

Rappaport, D. (2019). *Wilma's way home: The life of Wilma Mankiller* (L. Kuku, Illus.). Disney Hyperion.

Thompson, L. A. (2015). *Emmanuel's dream: The true story of Emmanuel Ofosu Yeboah* (S. Qualls, Illus.). Schwartz & Wade Books.

Tonatiuh, D. (2014). *Separate is never equal: Sylvia Mendez & her family's fight for desegregation* (D. Tonatiuh, Illus.). Abrams Books for Young Readers.

Tonatiuh, D. (2019). *Soldier for equality: José de la Luz Sáenz and the Great War* (D. Tonatiuh, Illus.). Abrams Books for Young Readers.

Winter, J. (2011). *The watcher: Jane Goodall's life with the chimps* (J. Winter, Illus.). Schwartz & Wade.

Winter, J. (2019). *Our house is on fire: Greta Thunberg's call to save the planet* (J. Winter, Illus.). Beach Lane Books.

Conclusion: Using Picture Books to Build a Lesson Plan

The tradition of storytelling dates back more than 32,000 years, with the earliest versions of stories told in cave paintings on the walls of the Chauvet-Pont d'Arc cave in southeastern France. The paintings spread across six rooms and show hundreds of animals, some dating back to the Ice Age, as well as red-ochre handprints, line drawings, and other abstract representations. Archeologists and prehistoric art experts believe the paintings in Chauvet-Pont d'Arc documented the people's experiences and were spiritual offerings to their deities.

Storytelling has evolved from these early paintings to encompass oral traditions, printed stories, multimedia presentations, and many other adaptations and advancements in the ways that stories are created, recorded, and shared. The purposes of stories have also broadened to serve many goals: to document life experiences, argue a perspective, entertain a crowd, educate students, and offer explanations for aspects of the world that are mysterious and terrifying. Storytelling defines and demonstrates the fundamental aspects of life: sharing, educating, debating, worshipping, mourning, and celebrating.

With such a wide breadth of focus and purpose, stories are a powerful tool to help children learn in a multitude of academic ways, from practicing the skills of reading, listening, and comprehending to learning details of subject knowledge. Picture books can provide information about core subjects, whether that is a historically important event or person, invention or discovery, or topic details explained in plots and through the dialogue and actions of the stories' protagonists.

The power of stories reaches far beyond language and subject content learning, as picture books create shared experiences and introduce new perspectives. As we read or listen to stories, we learn about experiences that can be comfortably familiar or entirely foreign to us. Through stories we can find shared emotions and reactions and be taught about differences and experiences outside of our previous knowledge. Children can learn about the motivations and impacts of people, which helps to shape their understanding of their own place in the world.

The social and emotional skills that are demonstrated and taught through the text and illustrations of picture books touch all areas of a child's life, from their emotions and interactions with others to their perspective, social- and self-awareness, and their sense of identity and responsibilities in the world. Through the actions of their characters, picture books demonstrate cognitive skills, such as executive functioning skills, problem-solving, task initiation, and time management.

The breadth and depth of content and SEL coverage that picture books provide make them an excellent bridge to connect subject content and SEL themes, as shown in Figure 9.1.

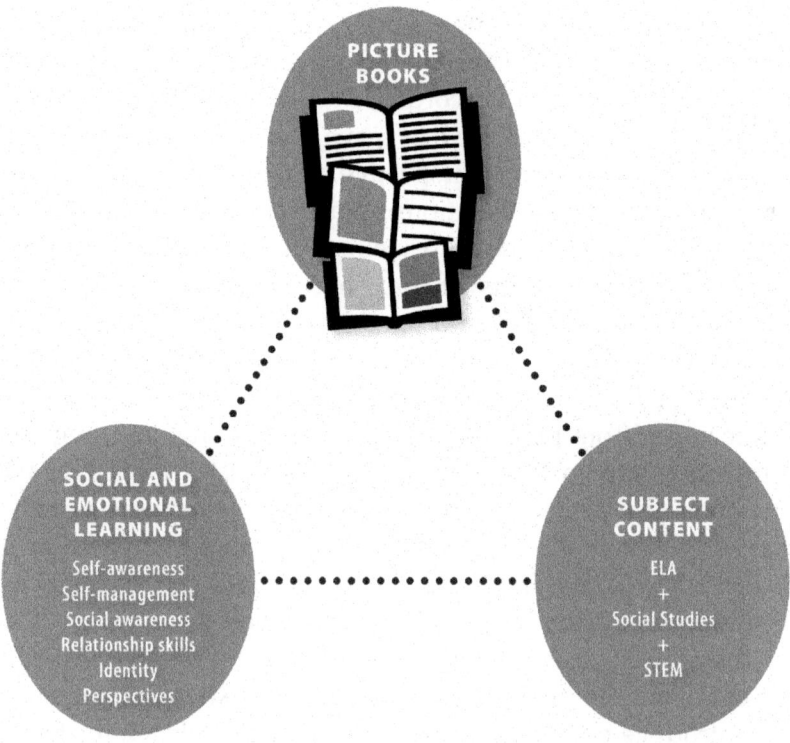

FIGURE 9.1 Connecting SEL Lessons and Subject Content With Picture Books
Source: Illustration Design by Melanie Bender Design

Teachers who cover multiple subjects in the same classroom or who do not have dedicated class periods for certain subjects, such as social studies or art, can put together cross-curricular lessons using a picture book as the foundation. For example, lessons on environmental movements and leaders cover both science and social studies concepts, and language arts lessons can use picture books on topics in STEM or social studies.

The ability to select picture books with differing reading levels, topics, lengths, and diversity of viewpoints provides educators with rich opportunities for differentiating the lesson. In mixed-ability classrooms with gifted, at-level, and below-level students, the lessons can use a mixture of picture books, including non-conforming books, wordless picture books, and high-low readers.

Building a lesson plan. Teachers can start with any of the three components—a picture book, a content topic, or an SEL domain—and then pull in the one or two of the other components. For example, teachers can start by selecting the content topic and relevant content standards. Table 9.1 lists the links to the relevant content standards for science, social studies, language arts, and STEM that teachers can consult in building the topic content and skills covered in the lesson plan.

Table 9.1 Selecting Subject Content and Standards for a Lesson Plan

Subject Content	Standards
Language Arts	Common Core English Language Arts—Informational text Common Core English Language Arts—Literature www.corestandards.org/ELA-Literacy/
Social Studies	National Council for the Social Studies: www.socialstudies.org/national-curriculum-standards-social-studies-chapter-2-themes-social-studies C3: www.socialstudies.org/standards/c3
Math	Common Core Mathematics: www.corestandards.org/Math/
Science	Next Generation Science Standards: www.nextgenscience.org/search-standards
Technology	ISTE: www.iste.org/standards/iste-standards-for-students

As the next step after selecting the core topic and relevant standards, a teacher could select a picture book related to the topic. Table 9.2 provides questions to think about when selecting a picture book for the lesson. Factors to consider include the quality of the book, the difficulty level and length, how well it matches with the challenges and strengths of the children who will read it, and whether it represents a diverse viewpoint.

Table 9.2 Selecting a Picture Book for a Lesson Plan

Criteria	Considerations
Overall Quality	Is it a quality book? • Rich themes or central ideas • Multifaceted characters or key individuals • Complex illustrations • Rich language • Multi-layered plot • Accurate (for informational texts) Do you like it? Are you excited to share the book with your students?
Topic and Theme Alignment	Does the topic align with the content area standards or serve as a base for the ELA standards? Does the theme align with the SEL domains or competencies you want to address?
Length	For a read-aloud, does the length match the attention span of the children in your classroom? For an independent or small group read, does this book provide the needed challenge or support (i.e., a longer book can challenge a stronger reader, and a shorter book can provide a more manageable task for a less-proficient reader)?
Complexity	Have you considered quantitative, qualitative, and reader/task factors to determine whether the book is a good fit?
Diversity	Do the chosen books represent the children in your classroom (i.e., mirrors)? Do the chosen books represent the diversity in broader society (i.e., windows)? Do the authors of the chosen books represent different areas of diversity (e.g., race, class, gender, language, religion, dis/ability)?

The final component to consider in building the lesson plan is the SEL domains and competencies that the teacher would like to cover in the lesson. Table 9.3 lists the Harvard Explore SEL domains and the CASEL competencies, along with examples of each.

Table 9.3 Selecting SEL Domains and Competencies for a Lesson Plan

Harvard Domains http://exploresel.gse.harvard.edu/compare-domains/	Examples
Cognitive	• Executive functioning skills • Good decision-making • Problem-solving • Working through challenges and learning from failure
Social	• Communicating, playing, and interacting with others • Managing conflicts
Emotion	• Understanding, expressing, and controlling emotions • Interpreting and appropriately responding to other children's emotions
Perspective	• Nurturing optimism, courage, gratitude, and hope • Developing a growth mindset, grit, and perseverance • Expanding self-confidence and willingness to step outside of comfort zones
Identity	• Fostering healthy self-awareness, self-efficacy, and sense of identity and place in the world • Developing an understanding of the diversity of identities within local and global communities
Values	• Developing ethical values, character traits, and habits that position a child to be a compassionate person who contributes to their community and world in positive ways

CASEL Competencies https://casel.org/sel-framework/	Examples
Self-management	• Managing emotions • Using self-discipline • Taking initiative • Demonstrating agency • Using planning and organizational skills
Self-awareness	• Identifying emotions • Examining prejudices and biases • Developing interests and a sense of purpose • Having a growth mindset

(Continued)

Table 9.3 (Continued)

CASEL Competencies https://casel.org/sel-framework/	Examples
Social Awareness	• Taking other people's perspectives • Demonstrating empathy, compassion, and gratitude • Identifying diverse social norms, including unjust ones
Responsible Decision-making	• Evaluating personal, interpersonal, community, and institutional impacts • Reflecting on one's role to promote personal, family, and community well-being • Demonstrating curiosity and open-mindedness • Identifying solutions for personal and social problems
Relationship Skills	• Communicating effectively • Demonstrating cultural competency

Sources: *CASEL'S SEL Framework: What are the core competence areas and where are they promoted?* (2020). CASEL. Retrieved from www.casel.org/what-is-SEL

Harvard EASEL Lab. (n.d.) Compare skill focus across frameworks. Harvard Explore SEL. Retrieved from http://exploresel.gse.harvard.edu/compare-domains/

Example: Building Out a Lesson Plan

As an example, to begin to build a lesson focusing on the Civil Rights Movement, teachers can start with the appropriate standards for Social Studies—the C3 Framework, which are linked to the Common Core ELA Standards, or the NCSS standards. C3 standards in the areas of Civics, such as (D2.Civ.8.K-2.) "Describe democratic principles such as equality, fairness, and respect for legitimate authority and rules," or History, such as (D2.His.3.K-2.) "Generate questions about individuals and groups who have shaped a significant historical change." These standards can also be linked to the ELA/Literacy Common Core Standards in areas such as reading, writing, and speaking and listening.

As a next step, teachers can select a book that is appropriate for the class on the topic of the Civil Rights Movement. In addition to considering the questions in Table 9.2, publisher and reviewer websites such as Kirkus (free), School Library Journal, and Publishers Weekly (both paid) provide helpful reviews of children's books that indicate target age levels and the quality of the book; starred reviews from any of those three sites are reliable indications that the book is high quality. School librarians are also an excellent source of advice for quality picture books for certain groups of students and on specific topics. A book's page on Amazon will often list excerpts from the three publishers and indicate whether the publishers gave the book a starred review under the "Editorial Reviews" section.

The selection of multiple books with varying reading levels, length, and focus offers an excellent opportunity to create a differentiated lesson plan, especially for a class with a variety of reading abilities. In the small-group or individual work portion of the lesson, a variety of books can be shared with the students and then discussed. This allows all students to contribute information from multiple perspectives while having a reading experience that is tailored to their needs and abilities.

As a last step, teachers can consider the SEL themes that are highlighted both in the topic of Civil Rights and in the picture books that will be used in the lesson. The plot points, illustrations, and dialogue of picture books about the Civil Rights Movement offer many entry points to SEL domains and competencies, including values, perspectives, identity, social awareness, and responsible decision-making. Biographies of Civil Rights leaders will demonstrate such characteristics as courage, hope, grit, and perseverance, as well self-management and responsible decision-making. Books that discuss the historical events will address social awareness aspects, such as identifying diverse social norms, including unjust ones.

Assessments and rubrics can incorporate various aspects of the lesson components, including the SEL portions, the book reading, and the subject content. Informal assessments can look at students' participation in the discussions, completion of the activities, and their work on any individual or small-group assignments, such as writing pieces, presentations, and artistic creations.

The use of picture books offers a wealth of choices and opportunities in lesson planning and facilitates the integration of SEL skills with content knowledge, offering opportunities to see and discuss SEL domains through the actions and dialogue of the characters. Picture books provide an excellent entry point for presenting and discussing the topic details in ways that are culturally relevant and academically tailored to a wide variety of students. Lessons can be differentiated to address all needs, including the needs of gifted and above-level students. The breadth and depth of characters, life experiences, and plot points in the picture books of the last two decades has expanded enormously, offering innumerable lenses through which to view the world—whether that is a world that is familiar and comforting or new and intriguing. For all of our readers, we hope that this book has given you some new ideas and ways to think about meeting all of your learners' academic and social and emotional needs.